Getting Skills Right

I0069126

Career Guidance
for Low-Qualified Workers
in Germany

OECD

BETTER POLICIES FOR BETTER LIVES

This work is published under the responsibility of the Secretary-General of the OECD. The opinions expressed and arguments employed herein do not necessarily reflect the official views of the Member countries of the OECD.

This document, as well as any data and map included herein, are without prejudice to the status of or sovereignty over any territory, to the delimitation of international frontiers and boundaries and to the name of any territory, city or area.

Please cite this publication as:
OECD (2022), *Career Guidance for Low-Qualified Workers in Germany*, Getting Skills Right, OECD Publishing, Paris, https://doi.org/10.1787/5e6af8da-en.

ISBN 978-92-64-95531-8 (print)
ISBN 978-92-64-79290-6 (pdf)
ISBN 978-92-64-87944-7 (HTML)
ISBN 978-92-64-41493-8 (epub)

Getting Skills Right
ISSN 2520-6117 (print)
ISSN 2520-6125 (online)

Foreword

The world of work is changing. Digitalisation, automation and globalisation are having a profound impact on the type and quality of jobs that are available and the skills required to perform them. The extent to which individuals, firms and economies can reap the benefits of these changes will depend critically on the ability of individuals to maintain and acquire relevant skills and adapt to a changing labour market over their working careers.

Career guidance for adults is a fundamental policy lever to motivate adults to train and help address the challenges brought about by rapidly changing skill needs. Such services are particularly important in the context of the COVID-19 pandemic and its aftermath, as many low-skilled adults risk losing their jobs and require assistance to navigate their career options in the changed labour market.

To explore this issue, the OECD Directorate for Employment, Labour and Social Affairs has undertaken an ambitious programme of work on the functioning, effectiveness and resilience of adult career guidance systems across countries. As part of this project, the OECD carried out an online survey in 11 countries (Argentina, Australia, Brazil, Canada, Chile, France, Germany, Italy, Mexico, New Zealand and the United States) to better understand the user experience of adults with career guidance, and any barriers adults might face in accessing these services. This report focusses on the results for Germany as well as on additional qualitative data collection focused on low-qualified adults. It also builds on the OECD's earlier reports *Career Guidance for Adults in a Changing World of Work* and *Continuing Education and Training in Germany* and leverages information on career guidance policies collected through a questionnaire sent to Ministries of Employment and Education and numerous interviews with key stakeholders.

This report was prepared by Karolin Killmeier from the Directorate for Employment, Labour and Social Affairs, under the supervision of Glenda Quintini (Skills team manager) and Mark Keese (Head of the Skills and Employability Division). Useful comments were provided by colleagues in the Skills and Employability Division in the OECD Directorate for Employment, Labour and Social Affairs.

This report is published under the responsibility of the Secretary General of the OECD. It was carried out with financial assistance from the JPMorgan Chase Foundation. The views expressed in this report should not be taken to reflect the official position of the JPMorgan Chase Foundation or OECD member countries.

Table of contents

FIGURES

INFOGRAPHICS

TABLES

Follow OECD Publications on:

http://twitter.com/OECD_Pubs

http://www.facebook.com/OECDPublications

http://www.linkedin.com/groups/OECD-Publications-4645871

http://www.youtube.com/oecdilibrary

http://www.oecd.org/oecddirect/

Acronyms and abbreviations

	General acronyms and abbreviations
AES	Adult Education Survey
AI	Artificial Intelligence
CET	Continuing education and training
COVID-19	Coronavirus disease 2019
BA	Federal Employment Agency
BAföG	Federal Training Assistance Act
BAMF	Federal Agency for Migration and Refugees
BBB	Educational Counselling and Career Guidance in Berlin
BBE	NRW's Guidance for Career Development
BIBB	Federal Institute for Vocational Education
BMAS	Federal Ministry of Employment and Social Affairs
BMBF	Federal Ministry of Education and Research
BMWi	Federal Ministry of Economy and Energy
DGB	German Trade Union Federation
DIE	German Institute for Adult Education
DIW	German Institute for Economic Research
ERDF	European Regional Development Fund
ESF	European Social Fund
EU	European Union
EUR	Euro
GDP	Gross Domestic Product
IAB	German Institute for Employment Research
IHK	Chamber of Commerce and Industry
ILO	International Labour Organization
ISCED	International Standard Classification of Education
ISCO	International Standard Classification of Occupations
LBB	Lifelong Vocational Guidance
LBBiE	Lifelong Vocational Guidance in employment
OECD	Organisation for Economic Co-operation and Development
NWS	National Skills Strategy
MAGS	Ministry of Employment, Health and Social Affairs of the State of NRW
MKW	Ministry of Culture and Sience of the State of NRW
MoBiBe	Mobile counselling on education and careers for refugees in Berlin
MWAE	Ministry of Economic Affairs, Labour and Energy of the State of Brandenburg
PES	Public Employment Services
PIAAC	Survey of Adult Skills
QCG	Skills Development Opportunities Act
SenIAS	Senate Department for Integration, Labour and Social Affairs of Berlin
SGB	Social Security Code
SMEs	Small and medium enterprises
VET	Vocational Education and Training
VHS	Adult Education Centres

Acronyms of the German federal states	
BW	Baden-Württemberg
BY	Bavaria
BE	Berlin
BB	Brandenburg
HB	Bremen
HH	Hamburg
HE	Hesse
NI	Lower Saxony
MV	Mecklenburg-Vorpommern
NW	North Rhine-Westphalia
RP	Rhineland-Palatinate
SL	Saarland
SN	Saxony
ST	Saxony-Anhalt
SH	Schleswig-Holstein
TH	Thuringia

Executive summary

In a changing world of work, job profiles constantly develop and the demand for skills and qualifications with them. Particularly, jobs that mainly involve simple and repetitive tasks are threatened by technology, which fosters demand for high-level cognitive skills and complex social interaction skills. Reskilling and upskilling initiatives, through continuing education and training (CET), could foster transitions to emerging sectors and occupations, but participation by low-qualified workers is low.

This study looks at the career guidance programmes available for low-qualified workers in Germany to help them navigate the ongoing changes and identify the most appropriate training and employment opportunities for them. In Germany, these services exist at national level and in the federal states and help adults overcome barriers to participating in CET or invest in their professional development. The report gives an overview of career guidance provision at the federal level and then describes career guidance needs and provision in the states of Berlin and North Rhine-Westphalia (NRW).

Prior to the COVID-19 pandemic, the labour market outcomes of low-qualified workers were good in Germany thanks to strong demand for these workers in several manufacturing and low-skilled service sectors. However, the need for social distancing, a temporary drop in consumer demand and disruptions in global markets and supply chains due to the pandemic have disproportionally affected low-qualified workers. While most economic indicators are close to their pre-pandemic level on average, the recovery is expected to be slower for this group. In addition, the labour market prospects of low-qualified workers are affected by structural changes.

Low-qualified workers are less likely to receive career guidance than those with higher qualifications, as employers focus their efforts in guidance and training on the high qualified. They are also less likely to receive training than those who are unemployed, as the public employment service systematically provides counselling to the unemployed. A range of multi-layered and interconnected barriers complicates the use among low-qualified workers, including finding time to attend counselling sessions, given their work and family responsibilities and scepticism or anxiety towards re-entering learning. Tackling these barriers requires individualised support, which is why the quality of career guidance plays an important role.

The career guidance offers differ significantly from one federal state to another in Germany. The Federal Employment Agency's (*Bundesagentur für Arbeit*, BA) new Lifelong Vocational Guidance in Working Life (*Lebensbegleitende Berufsberatung im Erwerbsleben*, LBBiE) aims at closing provision gaps. In addition, regional and sectoral networks intend to connect career guidance and CET providers with employers to plan and organise CET for employees better.

Policy recommendations

Streamline and connect existing guidance offers

- *Streamline current provision under a 'single brand' at national level:* Creating a nationwide brand can significantly improve the access to guidance provision, guarantee more consistent quality of services nationally and close provision gaps.

- *Ensure the sustainability of regional and sectoral networking initiatives:* Networking among career guidance and CET actors and companies is a promising strategy to encourage lifelong learning, especially for low-qualified employees.

- *Support existing career guidance offers at federal state level in engaging low-qualified workers:* Low-qualified workers need tailored career guidance services to address multiple barriers (e.g. lack of time, aversion to change, anxiety to return to classroom learning, financial or social barriers).

Strengthen outreach measures

- Outreach activities can help raise awareness of career guidance opportunities. Institutions that are already in contact with low-qualified adults could be leveraged to function as mediators.

Improve the framework conditions of career guidance services for low-qualified workers

- *Introduce guidance leave:* Policy makers in Germany are considering the harmonisation and expansion of nationwide CET leave and it should include the option to use the leave for guidance sessions.

- *Set-up one-stop-shops:* Guidance offers should help adults identify their professional development needs and matching CET opportunities, as well as address any other barriers they might face (e.g. financing, health issues, care responsibilities).

- *Integrate career guidance with the validation of skills and partial qualifications:* Establishing a working group composed of the key stakeholders in career guidance, validation of skills and CET could explore linkages between these three policy areas and issue recommendations.

Pursue the further development of the Public Employment Service (*Bundesagentur für Arbeit, BA*) towards a combined Public Employment <u>and</u> CET Service

- *Increase the capacities of Job Centres to provide career guidance:* The guidance needs of clients in the Job Centres are often high and their situations very complex. Caseworkers should be accompanied by specialised (LBBiE) counsellors and coaches to provide individualised support.

- *Grant flexibility in the use and combination of different delivery channels:* While digital and online guidance should continue to be used, low-qualified workers clearly prefer face-to-face guidance.

- *Collect and analyse data on guidance sessions and users:* While most co-ordinated guidance offers in the federal states collect and publish some data, no data is collected by the biggest nationwide provider of guidance, the BA.

Provide support to Small and Medium-sized Enterprises (SMEs) on providing career guidance and training for low-qualified employees

- *Target existing programmes for companies to support low-qualified workers:* Existing support programmes for companies should raise awareness of the importance of supporting lower qualified staff.

- *Guidance services for companies should go beyond the initial analysis and recommendations*: Support throughout the implementation process and with the administrative requirements is crucial to increase take-up.

Improve the quality of career guidance services

- *Implement a nationwide quality standard framework*: Such a framework should cover both the continuous development of a provider's internal processes and a competency profile for counsellors.

- *Set clear qualification requirements for career guidance counsellors:* This is particularly important when counsellors will be dealing with low-qualified adults facing multiple participation barriers.

- *Provide incentives for regular training of career guidance providers:* Counsellors need support to keep the abilities and knowledge required to work with low-qualified workers up to date.

- *Expand the use of AI solutions during the career guidance process*: While it is crucial that some components of career guidance are conducted by skilled counsellors, others could be automated leveraging advances in AI.

1 Low-qualified workers and their career guidance options in Germany

The COVID-19 pandemic and pre-existing structural trends put pressure on the low-qualified workforce, particularly those in jobs at high risk of automation, to reskill and upskill. Career guidance programmes can support this group in navigating CET offers, career options and sustainable job transitions. Advice can also target companies to support them in developing their skill development strategies and thus their employees' skills and opportunities. This chapter discusses i) the labour market opportunities and prospects of low-qualified workers in Germany; ii) current patterns of their participation in CET and career guidance; and iii) the available career guidance offers and networking initiatives at the federal level.

Introduction

In Germany, the three 'Ds' – Digitalisation, Decarbonisation and Demographic Change are dominating the headlines. Countless studies have analysed the impact of these megatrends on the world of work and documented how job profiles are changing. The impact of these megatrends is likely to be particularly large in Germany, where around 54% of all jobs are expected to undergo significant change or disappear entirely over the next 15 years, compared to 47% in the OECD on average (Nedelkoska and Quintini, 2018[1]).

When it comes to specific skill needs, the megatrends are generally strengthening the demand for high-level cognitive skills and complex social interaction skills, potentially leaving behind low-qualified adults working in jobs that are very intensive in simple and repetitive tasks (OECD, 2019[2]). Reskilling will be very important to prepare for these changes but adults in the jobs most at risk rarely participate in continuing education and training (CET), exposing them to a high risk of (long-term) unemployment due to skills obsolescence.

In response to these trends, many countries have developed career guidance programmes to support individuals and companies in navigating career options and sustainable job transitions (Box 1.1). Through these programmes, governments hope to maintain competitiveness, prevent increases in unemployment and foster inclusiveness. **In this context, this report provides an overview of the career guidance landscape in Germany with a particular focus on services that low-qualified workers can access and puts forward concrete recommendations on how to strengthen provision for this group.**

This report also covers publicly (co-)funded guidance for companies. Most training already takes place in the workplace but employers are less likely to provide training to their low-qualified employees than to those with high qualifications (OECD, 2021[3]). Helping companies to assess their own skills needs and invest in training for their employees is thus particularly important for low-qualified workers.

Lifelong learning and career guidance have received significant public attention in Germany in recent years. This materialised for example in programmes such as Learning Regions (*Lernende Regionen*, 2001-2008), Learning on Site (*Lernen vor Ort 2009-2014*), the Education Premium (*Bildungsprämie*, since 2008), the set-up of CET networks (*Aufbau von Weiterbildungsverbünden since 2020*) and, more recently, the Skills Development Opportunities Act (*Qualifizierungschancengesetz*, in 2019) and the Work of Tomorrow Act (*Arbeit-von-morgen-Gesetz*, in 2020). In addition, the coalition agreement of the recently formed government mentions the need to better network CET and guidance actors and to facilitate access to their services. While in theory stakeholders in politics and society agree that lifeong learning requires a neutral and interdisciplinary career guidance service, it is striking that there is no sustainable programme in Germany that draws low-qualified workers and provides services targeted at their needs to them. Small pilot projects have targeted adults in this group and often shown very positive results (see Chapters 2 and 3) but have not been scaled-up so far.

Low-qualified workers face a broad range of barriers to actively engage with career guidance providers and to develop their career plan and they need advice on how to overcome them. When approaching career guidance, adults in this group often face barriers related to a lack of awareness of existing services and their benefits, but also linked to scepticism towards training, limited finances or lack of time. Qualitative interviews conducted to accompany this report (see Annex B) suggest that guidance for low-qualified employees is most successful when it is holistic, i.e. when it helps adults navigate education and training offers as well as access other relevant services at the same time. This requires: i) skilled counsellors, who have sufficient time and resources to provide tailored assistance to each individual and to those who are not aware or remain sceptical of guidance offers; and ii) outreach activities to improve engagement. Existing guidance approaches fall short of these requirements, limiting participation by low-qualified workers. The current approach to solving this issue is to set up small-scale pilot programmes for sub-groups in certain regions, industries or occupations, but this approach creates support gaps for some groups. To address the needs of low-qualified workers, it is important to draw from the outcomes of successful pilots and adapt existing guidance structures.

The setup of career guidance offers in Germany varies considerably across federal states, resulting in unequal access and difficulties in navigating available services. In this context, a recent study published by the OECD (2021[4]).has already stressed the need to offer career guidance under a single brand. This report provides a brief overview of career guidance provision at the national level and goes on to analyse provision in two federal states: Berlin and North Rhine-Westphalia (NRW). They provide detailed examples of well-developed guidance offers and are therefore useful for other federal states and countries looking to improve career guidance service co-ordination.

The analysis conducted in this report draws from several sources, including virtual interviews with German stakeholders, quantitative employment statistics collected by the Federal Employment Agency (*Bundesagentur für Arbeit*, BA) and micro census data collected by the statistical offices of the federal states and the federation following the labour force concepts of the International Labour Organization, ILO (see Annex A). As mentioned above, the report also presents new insights from qualitative interviews on career guidance (QIG) that have been conducted with 50 low-qualified employees specifically for this study to learn more about their experiences with and their barriers towards the use of career guidance. In addition, it uses results of the online Survey of Career Guidance for Adults (SCGA) carried out by the OECD in 11 countries (Argentina, Australia, Brazil, Canada, Chile, France, Germany, Italy, Mexico, New Zealand and the United States) to better understand the experience of adults with career guidance and the barriers adults face in accessing career guidance services.

Box 1.1. The definition of career guidance used in this review

Career guidance refers to a range of services intended to assist adults to make well-informed educational, training and occupational choices and – in the short or longer term – to improve their employability. Services can include different activities such as the provision of information, personalised counselling, mentoring schemes, skills assessments, or group sessions.

Career guidance services aim to help people plan their careers in a long-term perspective, typically balancing professional and personal goals. They have the potential to strengthen skill development, facilitate labour market transitions and support a better match between the supply and demand of skills and labour. Adults have varying levels of knowledge about the labour market and training opportunities, as well as varying abilities to plan and visualise their futures. Career guidance can help address these inequalities. It may also support labour market inclusion of vulnerable groups by referring adults to relevant services, including training opportunities.

Source: OECD (2021[5]), *Career Guidance for Adults in a Changing World of Work*, https://doi.org/10.1787/9a94bfad-en.

The specific needs of low-qualified workers in Germany

In a country like Germany, where the economy is producing increasingly high-quality and knowledge-intensive goods and services, low-qualified workers risk losing their jobs with few options for re-employment. In hiring processes, Germany's labour market is also still strongly focused on a person's completed formal qualification. While this is slowly changing with the development of partial qualifications and micro credentials, it still makes access to high quality employment difficult for workers without a completed formal diploma.

Two definitions of what constitutes a low qualification are provided in Box 1.2. While the definition used in the Census is consistent with the international definition, the definition used by the German PES (*Bundesagentur für Arbeit*, BA henceforth) is based solely on having completed a vocational or higher education qualification, underscoring the importance of the dual vocational training system within the German education system.

Box 1.2. Definition of adults with low qualifications

Definition used in the micro census and in international comparison

Adults with low qualification levels are individuals whose highest educational attainment level is at most lower secondary education (ISCED 0-2) (*Geringqualifizierte*). In the German context, these adults have left education after compulsory comprehensive school or earlier (*Primär- und Sekundarbereich I*) and at most hold a lower secondary school certificate (*Realschulabschluss/ Mittlere Reife*). They have not completed a full vocational qualification.

Definition by the Bundesagentur für Arbeit (BA)

The term "persons with low qualifications" is not defined by law. The statistical delimitation of the group of persons follows § 81 Para. 2 No. 1 and No. 2 SGB III, according to which "persons with low qualifications" are to be understood as those employees who:

- do not have a vocational qualification for which a training period of at least two years is stipulated under federal or federal state law, or
- have a vocational qualification but have worked in a semi-skilled or unskilled job for more than four years, which makes them be considered to be no longer likely to be able to work in their profession (occupationally alienated).

As such, this definition includes a broad range of adults. In some cases, adults classified as low qualified by the BA have genuinely poor skills and labour market difficulties, notably: school drop-outs by the census definition (i.e. adults who have neither completed higher education – *Abitur* – nor a vocational qualification) or adults who return to the labour market after several years or parental leave. In other cases, adults classified as low qualified by the BA may possess higher qualifications that are not easily recognised in the labour market, notably adults who have completed higher education, adults without a vocational qualification who have long professional experience, and people with unrecognised qualifications acquired abroad. Adults without a vocational training degree are generally defined as "auxiliary workers" or "helpers" (*Hilfsarbeitskräfte* or *Helfer*) in Germany.

Source: OECD (2021[4]), *Continuing Education and Training in Germany*, https://doi.org/10.1787/1f552468-en; BA (2021[6]), *Glossar der Statistik der Bundesagentur für Arbeit*, https://statistik.arbeitsagentur.de/DE/Statischer-Content/Grundlagen/Definitionen/Glossare/Generische-Publikationen/Gesamtglossar.pdf?__blob=publicationFile&v=7.

Low-qualified workers faced a good labour market outlook prior to the pandemic

Up until 2020, a decade of robust economic growth in Germany had translated into very low unemployment rates and high employment growth, yielding high standards of living and high levels of well-being by OECD standards. In addition to an increasing demand for higher qualifications and skills described above, the buoyant economy also generated shortages in middle- and low-skilled jobs. This tight labour market held many advantages for low-qualified adults as employers were competing for workers from a smaller pool of available workers. This gave low-qualified adults stronger bargaining power in terms of wages and employment conditions. It also incentivised employers to invest in their existing staff in the form of certified training.

During the first wave of the COVID-19 pandemic, at the beginning of 2020, German real GDP initially dropped by more than 10 percentage points, similar to other OECD countries. This far exceeded the impact of the 2008/2009 global financial crisis (OECD, 2021[7]). However, economic output rebounded rapidly in the second half of 2020 and through 2021 but with some clouding of economic prospects in late 2021 and early 2022 as a result of the rapid spread of the omicron variant of the COVID-19 virus.

The prospects of low-qualified workers are affected by the pandemic and by structural trends

The need for social distancing, a temporary drop in consumer demand and disruptions in global markets and supply chains due to the pandemic have dampened employment growth more in certain sectors, occupations and regions than in others. Overall, German unemployment and employment are not expected to return to pre-pandemic levels before 2023. Low-qualified workers have been particularly affected by the pandemic as teleworking was not always possible for this group (OECD, 2021[8]). The recovery is also expected to be slower or more disrupted for this group as a whole, although temporary labour shortages have emerged for some low-skilled jobs in some sectors such as retail and hospitality.

The long-term prospects of low-qualified workers will also be negatively affected by a number of megatrends leading to a growing demand for high-level cognitive skills and complex social interaction skills (OECD, 2020[9]). Already before the pandemic, employment growth was much lower in occupations at high risk of automation than in occupations at low risk, where low-qualified workers are concentrated. For the time being, slow employment growth in jobs at high risk of automation has not yet led to a drop in the employment rate of low-qualified workers, largely because the number of workers with a low education has fallen in line with the demand for these workers (OECD, 2021[10]). As the labour market prospects of low-qualified workers are likely to deteriorate further, career guidance regarding training opportunities is key to improve their chances of transiting to more sustainable and better quality jobs.

Box 1.3. The urgency to focus on low-qualified adults varies from one federal state to another

Differences in the supply of and demand for low-qualified adults varies significantly across the federal states. As a result, while the need for low-qualified adults to upskill and reskill is relevant throughout the country, the urgency is much more pronounced in some federal states than in others.

On the supply side, on average, 14% of adults in Germany are low qualified. Yet, there are large differences in the share of low-qualified adults between federal states and by gender (Figure 1.1). The lowest share of low-qualified adults can be found in the Eastern German states Thuringia, Saxony, Mecklenburg-Vorpommern, Brandenburg and Saxony-Anhalt. They are also the only states, including Berlin, where there are fewer low-qualified women than men.

At the other end of the scale, NRW and Bremen have the highest shares of low-qualified adults, particularly among women. The share of low-qualified women varies between less than 5% in Thuringia and almost 22% in Bremen, and for men between 5% and 18% in the same federal states. The scope for investing in upskilling varies accordingly.

Figure 1.1. The share of low-qualified adults varies from one federal state to another

Share of adults with low qualification levels by gender, 2019, percentage

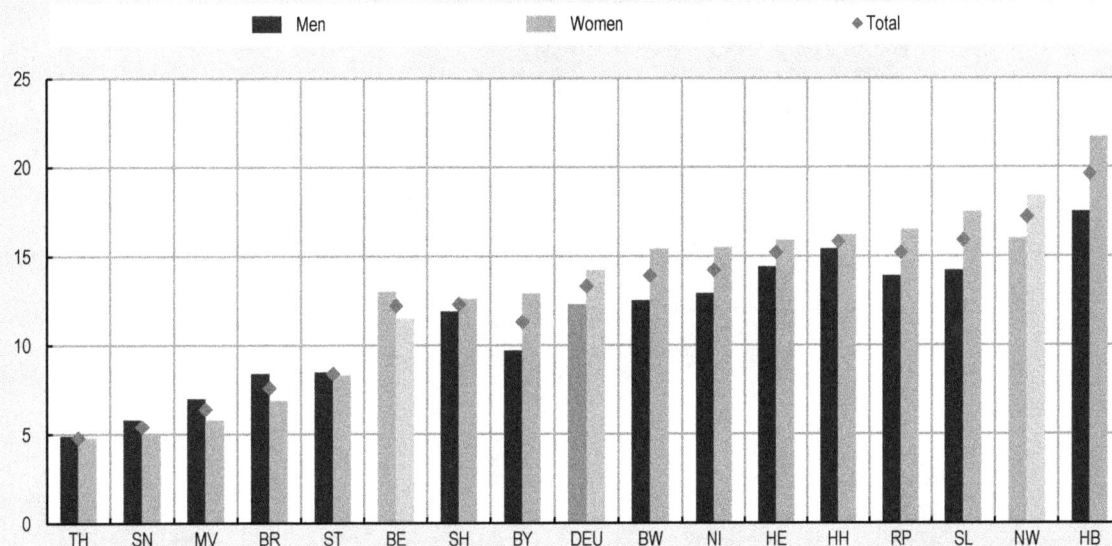

Note: Adults 25 to under 65-year-olds, who do not have an upper secondary qualification (without vocational qualification and without a higher education entrance qualification – ISCED 3) in the population of the corresponding age group.
Source: Statistical Offices of the Federal Government and the federal states, Micro census data 2019; Heinze et al. (2013[11]) *Strukturpolitik zwischen Tradition und Innovation – NRW im Wandel;* Elmshäuser (2016[12]), *Geschichte Bremens;* Zimmermann et al. (2009[13]), *NRW 2025: Vom Hort der alten Industrien zum Magnet der Moderne?*.

On the demand side, federal states are affected to different degrees by the structural changes brought about by the megatrends (Figure 1.2). The risk of job automation, for instance, varies widely, ranging from 27.1% in Mecklenburg-Vorpommern to 38.6% in Saarland.

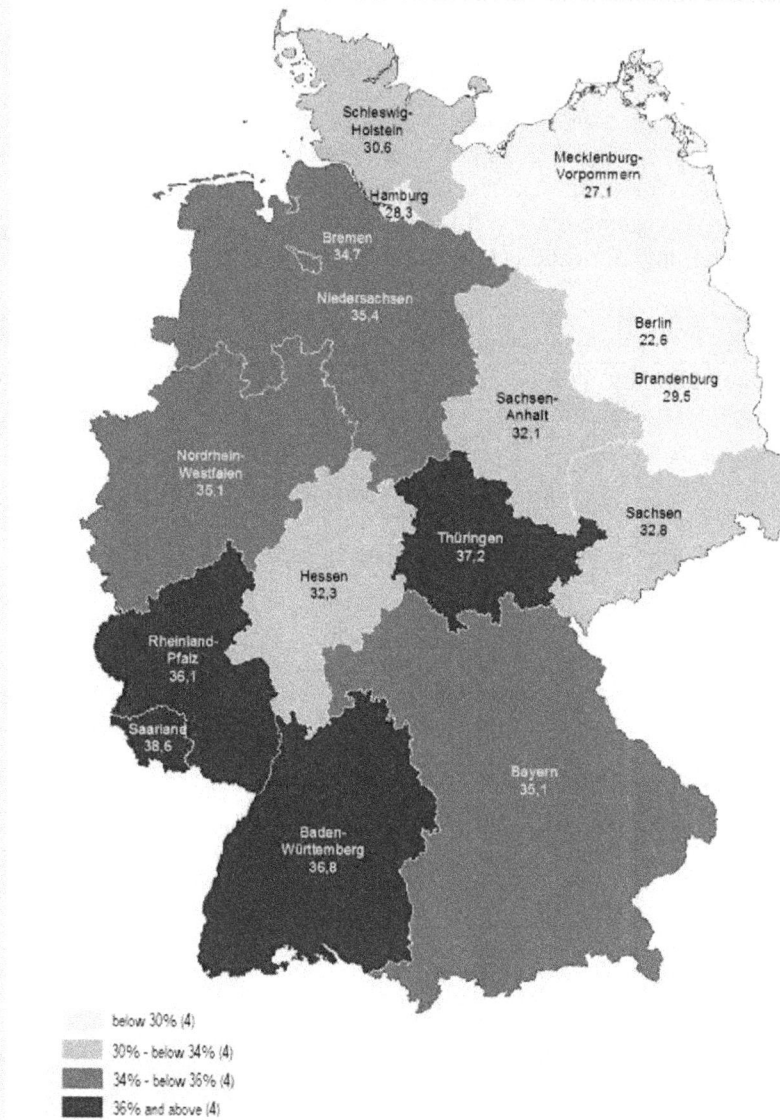

Figure 1.2. Different degrees of automation potential suggest varying degrees of urgency

Employees in jobs with high automation potential (> 70%) in the federal states, 2019

Note: Automation potential = share of activities that could already potentially be done by computers or computer-controlled machines today. Source: Dengler and Matthes (2021[14]), *Auch komplexere Tätigkeiten könnten zunehmend automatisiert werden*, IAB-Kurzbericht 13|2021, https://doku.iab.de/kurzber/2021/kb2021-13.pdf.

Low-qualified adults are also the least likely to participate in CET

The OECD's Priorities for Adult Learning Dashboard (PAL) looks at differences in CET participation between different socio-economic groups across OECD countries. Data is available for all adults, including workers. It shows that, on aggregate, Germany has some of the largest inequalities in CET participation in the OECD especially by qualification and skill levels. The 2018 AES data for Germany confirm that these gaps in participation remain large. Both data sources highlight particularly strong gaps between low-qualified adults and their high-qualified peers (OECD, 2021[4]). OECD analysis, based on the Survey of Adult Skills (PIAAC), suggests that the differences are very similar when restricting the analysis to employed adults.

The latest available data on low-qualified adults' participation in CET by federal states, including Berlin and NRW, date back to 2015 from the German micro census (Bertelsmann Stiftung, 2018[15]). The published data equally refers to adults, as opposed to workers only. To the question "Have you taken part in one (or more) further education or vocational training courses in the last 12 months?" 6% of low-qualified adults answered 'yes' compared with 12% among all adults. The likelihood that a low-qualified person would participate in CET was almost twice as high in Saxony-Anhalt (9%) as in North Rhine-Westphalia (5%). Participation in NRW is thus below average, while it is slightly above the national average in Berlin but remains very low.

Both NRW and Berlin would benefit from increased commitment to encouraging low-qualified adults, especially workers threatened by automation (Figure 1.2), to take up learning opportunities. Career guidance can play an important role in creating awareness and steering individuals towards suitable offers.

Low-qualified workers face multiple barriers to participation in CET

Low-qualified workers face multiple, multi-layered and interconnected barriers to participation. The academic literature on adult learning typically distinguishes between dispositional, situational and institutional barriers[1] (OECD, 2021[4]). Several studies have shed light on the barriers that the low qualified face in the uptake of CET, although they generally cover all adults, rarely focusing on workers only. Knowledge of these barriers – and ideally tools to overcome them – can considerably improve the quality of guidance. The barriers that low-qualified workers face are very different from those faced by workers with higher qualifications.

Looking at general findings for adults, the low qualified face, on average, a higher number of barriers to participation than those with higher qualifications. While adults with university degrees named one barrier to learning participation on average, low-qualified adults named close to three (Osiander and Stephan, 2018[16]). As described in detail below, institutional barriers are starker in some regions in Germany than in others. The National Skills Strategy (*Nationale Weiterbildungsstrategie*, NWS) has also acknowledged that existing gaps need to be closed and regions with weaker guidance offers need support to strengthen them.

Dispositional and situational barriers are highly individual for each adult. Nevertheless, several studies have found that dispositional barriers are more prevalent for low-qualified adults than for higher qualified adults (Osiander and Stephan, 2018[16]; BA, n/a[17]). This is in line with the finding that 67% of low-qualified German adults report the concern of "not being used to learning anymore" (OECD, 2021[4]).

One of the barriers that is most specific to low-qualified workers is the scepticism or anxiety towards re-entering a learning environment. The perception of not being able to learn anymore, fears of exams and of returning to a classroom environment and low confidence are reasons often cited by this target group for not participating. Data, referring to adults, show that not being used to learning is the most cited reason (67%) for not taking up CET among low-qualified adults according to an online survey by the German Institute for Employment Research (IAB), conducted in 2017 with 800 employees (Figure 1.3). This compares to 43% among adults holding a vocational training degree. Qualitative evidence is available specifically for low-qualified employees. The following quote from interviews with low-qualified employees commissioned in the context of this study (QIG) illustrates the barriers that exist to return to formal learning in particular:

> *I am not interested in opportunities for continuing education and training these days, because I am already a little bit older. It's not worth it. [...] They offered me a vocational training – but I said no, I am not going back to school. That doesn't work for me.*
>
> *49-year-old female hotel housekeeper*

Another frequently cited barrier for taking up training is the expectation that participation does not provide obvious and immediate benefits, such as financial benefits after completion, a promotion or another improvement in job quality. This expectation keeps them from even considering the different training options they have access to. The view that CET may not yield financial benefits after completion is the second most mentioned barrier (53% among low-qualified, 42% among those with a vocational degree) in the IAB's survey. Insights from the QIG highlight that career guidance for this group of adults may need to bring up considerations other than financial on the benefits of participation in training:

> *Someone once asked me 'how to you imagine your future, do you always want to earn so little money?' Yes, money is nice, but you know what you also need to consider is: do I enjoy it, do I want it? And you also have to consider if you are happy with your boss; does he deserve that you are leaving from one day to another?*
>
> *31-year-old male janitor*

The QIG suggest that low-qualified employees are also generally content with their work, working environment and employer and do not see enough reasons to initiate bigger changes to their current situation. This could reflect risk-aversion and a myopic attitude towards inevitable forthcoming change in their current jobs, which outreach activities and career guidance services would need to address. The following quotes illustrate the point that many low-qualified employees interviewed in the context of this study highlight the good working relationships with their boss and co-workers as key to the satisfaction with their work:

> *I enjoy the work. I like my boss and colleagues. It is a relaxed working atmosphere; you know what you got to do, but you can also ask questions if you are not sure. They explain things to you. […] I would like to continue working in this job, because I enjoy it and am interested in the profession.*
>
> *34-year-old male interviewee*
>
> *The job is very varied and you can implement your own ideas. The colleagues are nice. Even if clients are sometimes difficult, it is possible to handle.*
>
> *48-year-old female administrative assistant*

As such, what may look like lack of interest in participating in CET may be closely connected to the characteristics and preferences of this group. In addition, some situational barriers have been found to prevent or complicate the participation in training by low-qualified employees, such as frequent changes of work and employer and lack of time due to work schedules.

Tackling dispositional and situational barriers to training requires personalised holistic support…

Dispositional barriers are highly personal while situational ones require actions on several fronts, including timing, length and format of provision. For this reason, personalised and holistic support are crucial to valuable career guidance services for low-qualified workers.

The expertise of career guidance counsellors plays an important role in reaching out to low-qualified adults. To play a strong motivational role and address dispositional barriers, guidance advisors need to be well trained, well paid and equipped with the right tools, information and time to motivate and guide this target group. In addition, well-trained counsellors and coaches can accompany low-qualified adults to invest in their careers. In many cases, one-stop-shop settings have proven effective to address a combination of barriers.

The findings from the QIG interviews and quantitative data also point at the need to facilitate the recognition of prior learning and to direct adults in this group to modular and partial qualifications. Rather than achieving a full qualification in two or three years of training, partial qualifications could be completed step-by-step according to individual need and disperse worries about re-entering learning environments. As these systems are generally complex and not widely known, career guidance providers play a crucial role in supporting low-qualified workers throughout the process.

Establishing a first contact is often a challenge when workers do not search for career guidance themselves (OECD, 2021[4]). Around half of the low-qualified employees interviewed in the context of this study had looked for information on CET, typically online. Mobile services and outreach activities play a crucial role in overcoming barriers that keep adults from looking for career guidance.

Figure 1.3. Strong dispositional barriers call for high quality accompanying guidance

Self-reported reasons for not taking part in job-related education and training, by qualification level, 2017, percentage

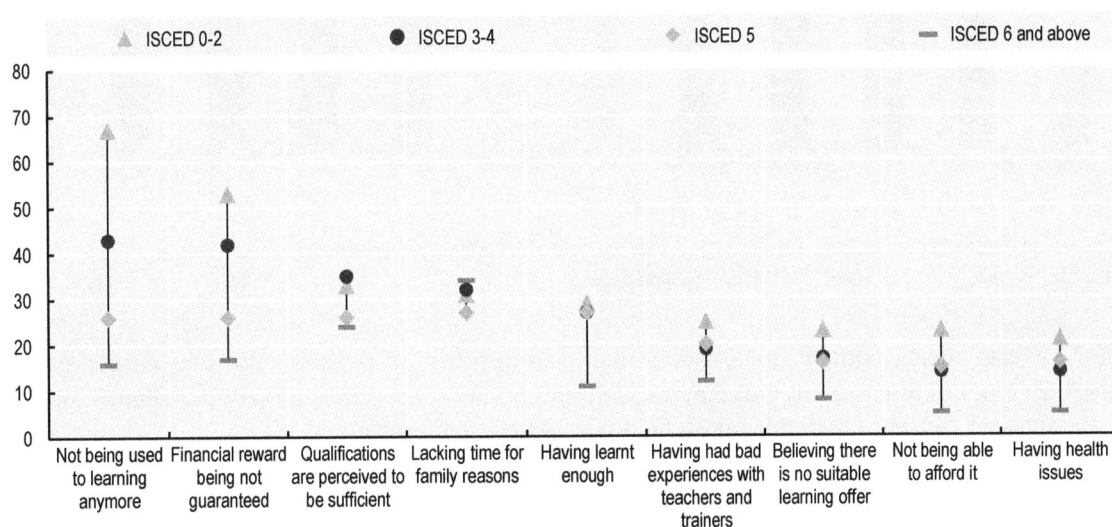

Note: ISCED 0-2 = No vocational qualification; ISCED 3-4 = Initial vocational degree (*Lehre/Ausbildung/Fachschule*); ISCED 5 = Graduate degree or vocational equivalent (*Meister/Techniker/Bachelor*); ISCED 6 = Post-graduate degree (*Master/Diplom* or higher). Low-qualified adults were underrepresented in the IAB survey. Results should not be considered representative for the German population.
Source: Osiander and Stephan (2018[16]), *Gerade geringqualifizierte Beschäftigte sehen bei der beruflichen Weiterbildung viele Hürden*, www.iab-forum.de/gerade-geringqualifizierte-beschaeftigte-sehen-bei-der-beruflichen-weiterbildung-viele-huerden, IAB-Forum; IAB online survey on CET.

...but the use of career guidance is limited

Despite the need for support to overcome barriers to CET participation, the OECD Survey of Career Guidance for Adults SCGA finds that less than 39% of low-qualified workers in Germany used a career guidance service in the five years prior to the survey compared to 55% among high-qualified workers (Figure 1.4).

Figure 1.4. Low-qualified workers use career guidance less

Percentage of workers who have spoken with a career guidance advisor over the past five years, by qualification level

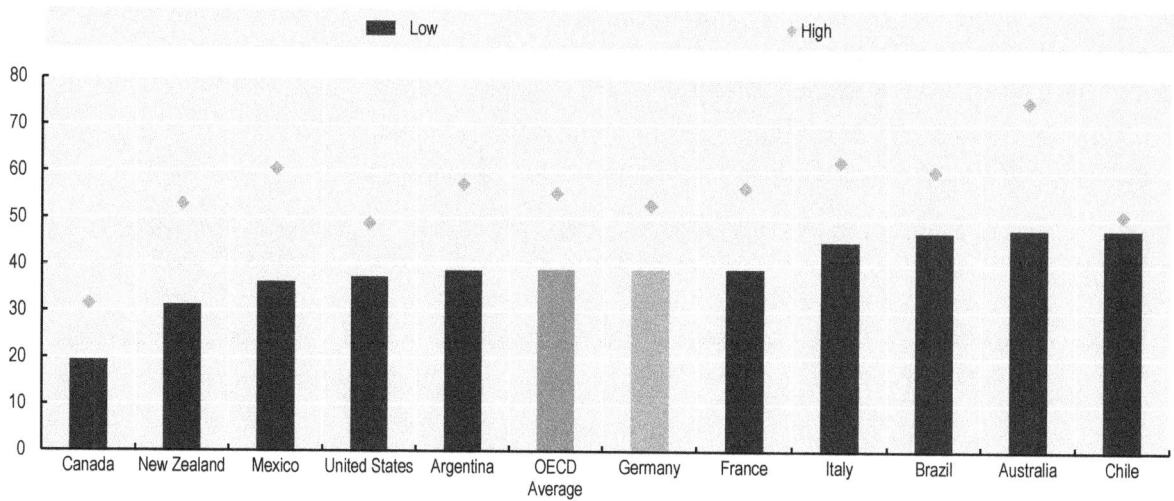

Note: The low educated group includes adults with a low or medium level of education (i.e. less than a bachelor's degree).
Source: OECD 2020/21 Survey of Career Guidance for Adults (SCGA).

The SCGA also sheds light on the reasons why low-qualified workers do not use career guidance (Figure 1.5). Most of them report that they do not feel the need for guidance. The qualitative interviews (QIG) do suggest, however, that this may hide a number of other barriers.

Figure 1.5. Low-qualified workers seem to not feel the need for career guidance

Percentage of low-qualified workers who did not speak with a career guidance advisor over the past five years, by reason

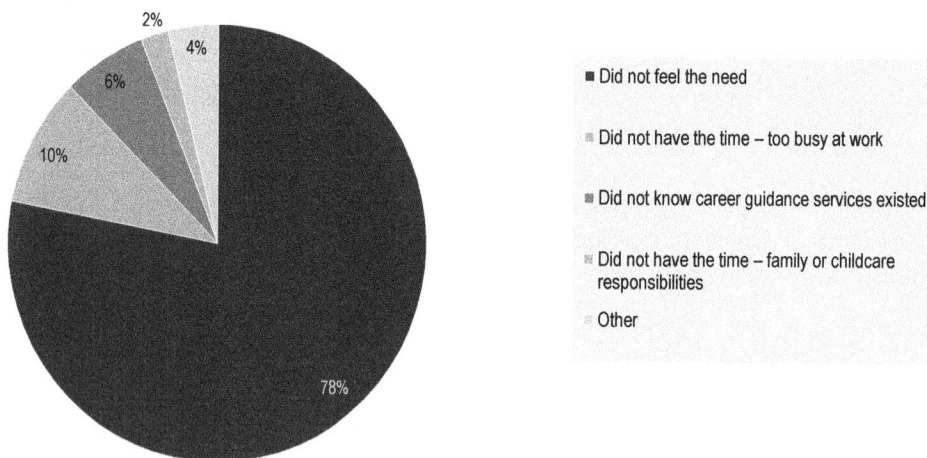

Note: The low educated group includes adults with a low or medium level of education (i.e. less than a bachelor's degree).
Source: OECD 2020/21 Survey of Career Guidance for Adults (SCGA).

Career guidance provision in Germany – structure and networks

The provision of career guidance for employed adults is limited at the federal level, with most guidance activities being co-ordinated at federal state level. BA's Lifelong Vocational Guidance service (*Lebensbegleitende Berufsberatung*, LBB), which is still being rolled-out in many regions, is the only face-to-face career guidance programme available consistently throughout the country. The LBB aims to shift the BA's approach from employability in the short term to supporting individuals in career planning and decision-making over the life-course. In addition to its branch focusing on students, the section focusing on employed adults is called Lifelong Vocational Guidance in working life (*Lebensbegleitende Berufsberatung im Erwerbsleben*, LBBiE).

The programmes CET Guide and CET Telephone (*Weiterbildungsratgeber / Weiterbildungstelefon*) by the Federal Ministry of Education and Research (*Bundesministerium für Bildung und Forschung*, BMBF) are also available everywhere in Germany but services are limited to career guidance online and via telephone. Social partners, the Adult Education Centres (*Volkshochschulen*, VHS) and universities provide career guidance everywhere in Germany. However, despite their nationwide presence, they are often governed in a decentralised way, with significant differences between local branches and federal states (OECD, 2021[4]). None of these services include an outreach or mobile component.

As a consequence of Germany's career guidance landscape that has grown organically over time and differs substantively across federal states, several networking initiatives aim at increasing exchange and co-ordination between the regions and at sharing learnings among the different actors at local, regional and national level. What is, however, still lacking in Germany is a nationwide initiative on career guidance that takes on the co-ordination between federal states and regions and sets out a global vision on career guidance for all stakeholders to follow.

Career guidance programmes exist in all federal states but the degree of co-ordination in provision varies

Career guidance programmes are available in all federal states in Germany (Table 1.1). Each federal state has its own online platform that serves as a single entry point to information on guidance. However, the degree to which these offers are integrated into an actual guidance network differs significantly, creating inequalities between the federal states. The offers fit into three different approaches to the provision of career guidance. A first group merely presents all career guidance providers in the federal state on one website, in some cases including offers by social partners, VHS, private providers and others. Offers in a second group follow a more centralised approach, with a responsible body, for example a ministry, that co-ordinates a network of subcontracted providers following an official call for tenders. This is the approach used in Berlin and NRW. The third approach is followed by federal states that provide career guidance through one specialised agency, not a network of independent organisations. The agencies may have one or several offices across the federal state, with varying numbers of career guidance staff at each office. This approach is often found in city-states.

In addition, some federal states have set up career guidance offers for specific target groups including women, refugees, parents, individuals re-entering the labour market who may benefit the most from additional guidance and from the focus on their particular needs. So far, none of these initiatives provide services that are adapted to the specific needs of low-qualified workers.

Table 1.1. Career guidance offers for adults in the federal states

Federal State	Original name	English name	Actors involved (incl. funders)	Target group	Guidance channel	Guidance offices
BW	Landesnetzwerk Weiterbildungs-beratung	Federal state network on CET guidance	VHS federation Baden-Württemberg, Ministry of Culture, Youth and Sport	Individuals	Face-to-face, chat, telephone, video call	74*
BY	Komm weiter in B@yern	Get ahead in Bavaria	Bavarian State Ministry for Family, Labour and Social Affairs	Individuals, companies	Online	-
BE	Berliner Beratung zu Bildung und Beruf	Berlin guidance on education and profession	Berlin Senate Administration for Integration, Employment and Social Affairs, k.o.s. GmbH	Individuals, SMEs	Face-to-face, telephone, video call, chat, e-mail	10
BB	Weiterbildung Brandenburg	CET Brandenburg	ESF, Wirtschaftsförderung Brandenburg GmbH (WFBB), Land Brandenburg	Individuals, companies, providers	Face-to-face, telephone, e-mail, chat	1
HB	Weiter mit Bildung und Beratung Bremen	Ahead with education and guidance	ESF, Chamber of employees Bremen, city of Bremen, IQ Network	Individuals, companies	Face-to-face, telephone, e-mail, video call	2
HH	Weiterbildung Hamburg	CET Hamburg	Authority for school and vocational training Hamburg	Individuals	Face-to-face, telephone, e-mail, fairs	15
HE	Bildungsberatung Hessen	Education guidance Hessen	ESF, Weiterbildung Hessen e.V., Land Hessen	Individuals	Face-to-face	124*
HE	Hessencampus (HC)	Hessencampus (HC)	Hessian Ministry of Education and Cultural Affairs	Individuals	Face-to-face	17
MV	Weiterbildung MV	CET in MV	ESF, Verein zur Förderung der Weiterbildungs-Information und Beratung e.V.	Individuals, companies	Face-to-face, telephone, chat	1
NI	Bildungsberatung in Niedersachsen	Education guidance in Lower Saxony	Lower Saxony Agency for Adult and Further Education, Association for Free Adult Education, Ministry for Science and Culture	Individuals	Face-to-face, video call, chat, e-mail	12
NRW	Weiterbildungs-beratung in Nordrhein-Westfalen	CET guidance in North Rhine-Westphalia	ESF, NRW Ministry of Labour, Health and Social Affairs, Gesellschaft für innovative Beschäftigungsförderung mbH (G.I.B.)	Individuals, SMEs	Face-to-face, telephone, webmail, events	250+
RP	Weiterbildungs-portal Rheinland-Pfalz	CET portal Rhineland-Palatinate	Rhineland-Palatinate Ministry of Science, Continuing Education and, and Culture and Ministry of Economics, Transport, Agriculture and Viticulture	Individuals, companies	Online resources	-
SH	Beratungsnetz Weiterbildung Schleswig-Holstein	Guidance net CET Schleswig-Holstein	ERDF, Schleswig-Holstein Ministry of Economy, Transport, Labour, Technology and Tourism, ver.di-Forum Nord, oncampus GmbH, Arbeit und Leben Schleswig-Holstein e.V., FuE-Zentrum FH Kiel GmbH and others	Individuals	Face-to-face, phone, e-mail, WhatsApp	7

Federal State	Original name	English name	Actors involved (incl. funders)	Target group	Guidance channel	Guidance offices
SL	Weiterbildungs-portal Saarland	CET portal Saarland	Saarland Ministry of Economic Affairs, Labour, Energy and Transport (MWAEV), Ministry of Education and Culture (MBK), Saarland Chamber of Labour (AK)	Individuals, companies, providers	Online resources	-
SN	Bildungsmarkt Sachsen	Education market Saxony	Saxon State Ministry for Economic Affairs, Labour and Transport, Sandstein Neue Medien GmbH	Individuals, providers	Online resources	-
ST	Fachkraft im Fokus	Skilled worker in focus	ESF, Saxony-Anhalt Ministry of Labour, Social Affairs and Integration	Individuals, companies	Online resources	-
TH	Bildungsportal Thüringen	Education Portal Thuringia	Thuringian universities	Individuals	Online resources	-

Note: * Mumber of member organisations.
Source: OECD (2021[4]), *Continuing Education and Training in Germany*, https://doi.org/10.1787/25206125.

The public employment service offers the only federal career guidance programme covering employed adults

The BA's responsibilities for guidance are defined in the Third Book of the Social Security Code (§ 29 SGB III following), which was adjusted/ expanded via the 2019 Skills Development Opportunities Act (*Qualifizierungschancengesetz*). In § 30 SGB III it defines the BA's mandate for guidance to improve individual employability and the development of individual career prospects, including for employees. This Act enabled the BA for the first time to introduce lifelong vocational guidance (*Lebensbegleitende Berufsberatung, LBB*), including for employed adults (*LBB im Erwerbsleben*, LBBiE) at any point in their careers (see Box 4.3 in (OECD, 2021[4])). The BA envisages LBBiE to complement existing programmes in the federal states rather than introducing a rigid nationwide model. While this allows integration with and adaptation to well-established programmes in the different states, it is also likely to accentuate existing differences between states without fostering much-needed co-ordination mechanisms.

The nationwide rollout of the LBB approach in co-ordination with the relevant ministries of the federal states was completed in January 2021. However, integration with local programmes is still ongoing in many federal states. Four hundred and fifty LBB advisors are being hired or trained between 2020 and 2022. LBB advisors are not present in each local offices of the BA: Each labour market region has a team of 10-20 LBB staff, who can be placed in selected local offices from where they can provide guidance in person, via telephone or video call (BA, 2019[18]). There is no specific distinction between advisors for services provided to students or to employees (LBBiE). LBB is financed by employees' and employers' unemployment insurance contributions.

There is currently no data on how many adults have received career guidance through LBB, or on the duration of the sessions, the waiting times to receive an appointment or any other data related to guidance provision. Information from the QIG conducted in the context of this study suggest that about two in five low-qualified interviewees have been contacted by the federal employment agency for career guidance purposes. The type of guidance services and the satisfaction with the guidance that was provided varied strongly between interviewees:

> *I spoke to the people from the federal employment agency/ the job centre [...] I spoke to them about what I wanted to do and that I hadn't found my path yet. [...] They also forwarded me to a different career guidance service, which discussed my professional goals with me, helped me find vacancies and draft applications.*
>
> *35-year-old male district helper*

> *First there was the job centre [...] they are responsible to help people find a job and to what extent (financial) support is available [...] Then I took part in a vocational preparation measure, which provided an overview of different occupations.*
>
> *23-year-old female salesperson*

> *One week ago I got a call from a lady at the job centre [...] She asked what my plans are after I finish school and I told her about my plans to become an emergency paramedic. She didn't ask for an appointment, she just asked questions about my professional future. [...] What I didn't like is that they are trying to encourage me to find a different professional path.*
>
> *21-year-old male first-aid assistant*

Social partners, Adult Education Centres and other education providers offer career guidance nationwide

Social partners, such as the Chambers of Commerce and Industry (IHK), local Chambers of Skilled Crafts or professional organisations and trade unions offer some guidance schemes that are available nation-wide. However, depending on the organisational setup and the degree of independence at the local level, the guidance offers and channels can differ considerably between federal states and communes.

Also the Adult Education Centres (VHS) provide career guidance across Germany.[2] Several low-qualified individuals interviewed in the context of this study had received guidance services through the VHS. They were typically sign-posted by other institutions, e.g. rehabilitation centres, job centres, to the guidance offer of the VHS. A positive experience of such guidance experience is provided below:

> *I first thought what kind of conversation will this be. They will just tell me that I haven't managed very much in my life to date. I was surprised myself that this guidance conversation [with the VHS] took such a positive turn. I finally learnt that there is someone who is not focusing on the negatives, but someone who first asks me: who are you, what do you have, what do you want? [...] I think you could attract many individuals with this kind of offer.*
>
> *46-year-old male interviewee working in retail*

Other public and private education and training providers also provide career guidance services, including to low-qualified workers, and often do so on behalf of the federal public employment services.

Support for companies to provide career guidance is also available

An important share of career guidance and training for adults happens in companies. According to data from the SCGA, almost 17% of adults in Germany who received career guidance did so through individual employers or employer organisations. Staff associations are obliged by law to provide career guidance to employees in Germany (OECD, 2021[4]). Employers also have an intrinsic interest in keeping their employees' skills up to date with the objective to stay competitive and foster innovation within the company. In-house training and career guidance are also a signal of appreciation to the employees and increase the attractiveness of the employer. Despite this self-interest, some firms may need support to deliver career guidance to their employees. The provision of career guidance and training require an analysis of individual skill development needs and expertise in the organisation of career guidance and training. SMEs, in particular, tend to lack the necessary capacity. Furthermore, when employers do provide career guidance and training, they are less likely to provide guidance to low-qualified employees or to employees in jobs at high risk of automation than to their higher-qualified peers (OECD, 2021[3]). Well-designed policies can assist companies with the implementation of skill development strategies that include career guidance services (OECD, 2021[4]).

Evidence from the QIG provides insights on the extent to which low-qualified employees are interested in receiving career guidance through their employers or if they would rather receive this guidance through other channels. Opinions vary, with half of the interviewees being positive about receiving guidance from their employer or at least open to the possibility. Those in favour typically emphasised the benefits of leveraging the relationship with their current employers and their knowledge of the context for the provision of career guidance:

> *It depends on what position one holds and what the opportunities are [...] When there are development opportunities within an enterprise it makes sense to receive guidance from an employer [...] An external guidance counsellor has nothing to do with the company and may misunderstand the situation. I would rather discuss with the employer directly.*
>
> *40-year-old female interviewee working in transport services*

The other half of individuals interviewed were not interested in career guidance provided through employers, notably because of a lack of trust, the perception that advice would not be independent and that it may focus on company – rather than individual – needs:

> *I don't think that guidance conversations between employee and employer can be open and truthful. Many employers – in particular in elderly care – expect that one continues working for them [...] but opportunities and wages may be better elsewhere.*
>
> *20-year-old female interviewee working in elderly care*

Several support initiatives for companies exist at the national level in Germany (see Table 4.5 in OECD (2021[4])). Some of these are part of broader public strategies to support enterprises, focusing for example on the quality of work (*unternehmensWert: Mensch* within *INQA* by the Federal Ministry of Employment and Social Affairs, BMAS) or artificial intelligence (*KI Strategie* by BMBF, BMAS and BMWi). Social and economic partners also play an important role in the provision of advice on CET to companies. In addition, trade unions and employer organisations provide advice to companies in the form of information material, conferences or seminars on-site via their staff associations.

The BA has its own offer for companies, the Counselling for Upskilling Programme for Companies (*Qualifizierungsberatung für Unternehmen*) which has been in place since 2013. It is one of the most comprehensive advice programmes for companies with a focus on SMEs. Specially trained BA consultants support employers with a tool for demographic staff analysis, assessment of training needs, selection of training providers and appropriate learning forms, and tracking the effects of training. The programme is modularised, i.e. companies can run through some or all of the modules available. In addition, all companies can access advice on different labour market topics provided by the BA (*Arbeitsmarktberatung*) free of charge. The guidance for companies is part of the wider training strategy (*WEITER.BILDUNG! – die Qualifizierungsoffensive*), initiated by BMAS.

Via this programme, the BA has already established connections with companies in many regions. This network could now be leveraged within the LBBiE to reach out to employees and especially to low-qualified employees, who are difficult to reach through standard career guidance outreach channels. So far, low-qualified adults are not a specific target group of any of the programmes, despite them being least likely to receive career guidance or training from their employer.

The NWS mentions the need to assess whether the support for companies provided by the BA and the support programmes of the federal states could be better linked, although no further commitment is made to establish these linkages in practice (OECD, 2021[4]).

Literacy initiatives provide another opportunity to deliver career guidance

The number of adults with low literacy levels, of whom the majority is also formally low qualified, remains stubbornly high in Germany. Many programmes, at all government levels, have tried to increase the participation of this target group in training. Today, literacy courses are mostly offered by Adult Education Centres (VHS) as well as by some other for profit and non-profit providers and are accompanied by career guidance services, to encourage potential learners to take up literacy courses. An overview of the providers and networks of literacy courses and guidance can be found in OECD (2021[4]). The Berlin's Centre for Basic Education (*Grund-Bildungs-Zentrum Berlin, GBZ*) is described in more detail in Chapter 2.

In addition, the overarching National Decade for Literacy and Basic Skills (*AlphaDekade*) was set up in 2016. This initiative brings together the federal government (BMBF), the federal states and a range of partners, including the BA, education providers, scientific institutions, social and economic partners, interest organisations, foundations, and representatives of municipalities. Its objective is to improve adults' reading and writing skills. Between 2016 and 2026, the Decade aims to implement activities in five areas: i) raising awareness; ii) research; iii) provision; iv) professionalisation of adult educators; and v) establishment of structures. Under the umbrella of the Decade, separate projects will take place, each funded by the federal government or the federal states.

More details about the implementation at the federal state level are given in Chapters 2 and 3. Most federal states have established a co-ordination office that connects the different actors in the area of basic CET. In NRW, for example, the office is located in the federal state's Association of Adult Education Centres (*Landesverband der Volkshochschulen*).

Networks play a central role in strengthening career guidance on CET

Providers, facilitators and organisers of career guidance have a long tradition of engaging with each other through different forms of networks. Networks have been created at different administrative levels, as well as by civil society organisations and providers themselves. A detailed presentation of the networks in Berlin and NRW can be found in the respective sections below and an overview of all networks at federal state-level can be found in OECD (2021[4]).

A recently developed initiative under the auspices of BMAS is the **Federal programme for the development of continuing education and training networks** (*Bundesprogramm zum Aufbau von Weiterbildungsverbünden*). The objective of this initiative is to open up new ways for SMEs to access CET for their employees. SMEs often struggle to organise and fund CET for their employees, which is why employees in SMEs are known to train less than their peers in bigger companies. To achieve this objective, the networks connect SMEs with CET providers, career guidance providers, chambers of commerce, the BA and other institutions active in the adult learning environment, ideally from the same sector or the same region. As such, the networks address several barriers to training at the same time. The networks draw the attention of HR managers, company owners and works councils to the growing need for CET in the wake of intensifying shortages of skilled workers. More specifically, the networks are then meant to co-ordinate CET and career guidance needs of different SMEs, organise joint CET and guidance provision at shared costs as well as to share best practices and information.

Concretely, BMAS provides funding for the creation of networks. Funding is allocated following a call for tender. Several CET networks have been set up since the end of 2020. A large number of expressions of interest during the call for tenders suggest that the demand for such support is high (BMAS, 2021[19]). In total, the budget will allow for public support of 39 networks. In addition, another programme was launched that will follow the same idea but with a specialisation on the automotive industry. The funding supports the creation of a co-ordination office for each network that is responsible for building up the network. This office can be, for example, in an economic development agency, within an education provider or even within an SME. While the programme is designed to encourage SMEs to train their employees, it also encourages bigger companies to foster CET along their value chains. The new CET networks will also focus on retraining employees for a change of sector. In addition, a central co-ordination centre will be set up for all CET networks. This will ensure an efficient exchange of knowledge and best-practice transfer between the individual networking initiatives.

In practice, a pilot network in Baden-Wuerttemberg, run by the federal state of Baden-Wuerttemberg and the BA, has shown that it takes time to develop the structures and the trust necessary to co-operate effectively on the above-mentioned objectives. It is therefore important to ensure the longevity of networks and to identify options to ensure their continuity early on. Other lessons could be drawn from similar programmes in Austria (*Impuls-Qualifizierungsverbund*) and the Netherlands (*MKB!dee*), where evaluations may be published earlier.

For individuals with a migration background, the initiative **Integration through Qualification** (*Integration durch Qualifizierung,* IQ) is a co-operative approach funded by BMAS and ESF and involving the Federal Agency for Migration and Refugees (BAMF), BMBF and BA introduced in 2005. The programme aims at improving labour market opportunities for people with a migration background. Sixteen IQ networks (*IQ Netzwerke*), one in each federal state, have been set up to improve and facilitate co-ordination among the different labour market actors to integrate the target group in the labour market. The networks have defined four priority areas for action: i) counselling for the recognition of qualifications acquired abroad; ii) adjustment qualifications; iii) intercultural competence development of key labour market actors; and iv) counselling for employers on hiring and integrating individuals with a migration background (IQ Netzwerk, 2021[20]). Examples for the concrete implementation of the networks can be found in the Chapters 2 and 3 of this report.

References

BA (2021), *Glossar der Statistik der Bundesagentur für Arbeit (BA)*, https://statistik.arbeitsagentur.de/DE/Statischer-Content/Grundlagen/Definitionen/Glossare/Generische-Publikationen/Gesamtglossar.pdf?__blob=publicationFile&v=7. [6]

BA (2019), *Weisung 201912024 vom 29.12.2019 - Lebensbegleitende Berufsberatung - Fachliche Umsetzung der Berufsberatung im Erwerbsleben*, http://www.arbeitsagentur.de/datei/ba146210.pdf. [18]

BA (n/a), *Rückmeldungen der AA/JC zu Geringqualifizierten und Qualifizierung*. [17]

Bertelsmann Stiftung (2018), *Deutscher Weiterbildungsatlas - Teilnahme und Angebot in Kreisen und kreisfreien Städten*, http://dx.doi.org/10.11586/2018057. [15]

BMAS (2021), *Das Bundesprogramm "Aufbau von Weiterbildungsverbünden" - Übersicht zu den geförderten Projekten*, http://www.bmas.de/DE/Arbeit/Aus-und-Weiterbildung/Weiterbildungsrepublik/Weiterbildungsverbuende/weiterbildungsverbuende-art.html. [19]

Dengler, K. and B. Matthes (2021), *Auch komplexere Tätigkeiten könnten zunehmend automatisiert werden*, https://doku.iab.de/kurzber/2021/kb2021-13.pdf. [14]

Elmshäuser (2016), *Strukturpolitik zwischen Tradition und Innovation — NRW im Wandel; Geschichte Bremens*, C.H.Beck. [12]

Heinze, R. et al. (2013), *Strukturpolitik zwischen Tradition und Innovation — NRW im Wandel*, Springer-Verlag. [11]

IQ Netzwerk (2021), *Landesnetzwerke*, http://www.netzwerk-iq.de/foerderprogramm-iq/landesnetzwerke. [20]

Nedelkoska, L. and G. Quintini (2018), "Automation, skills use and training", *OECD Social, Employment and Migration Working Papers*, No. 202, OECD Publishing, Paris, https://dx.doi.org/10.1787/2e2f4eea-en. [1]

OECD (2021), *Career Guidance for Adults in a Changing World of Work*, Getting Skills Right, OECD Publishing, Paris, https://dx.doi.org/10.1787/9a94bfad-en. [5]

OECD (2021), *Continuing Education and Training in Germany*, Getting Skills Right, OECD Publishing, Paris, https://doi.org/10.1787/1f552468-en. [4]

OECD (2021), *OECD Economic Outlook, Volume 2021 Issue 1*, OECD Publishing, Paris, https://dx.doi.org/10.1787/edfbca02-en. [7]

OECD (2021), *OECD Employment Outlook 2021: Navigating the COVID-19 Crisis and Recovery*, OECD Publishing, Paris, https://dx.doi.org/10.1787/5a700c4b-en. [8]

OECD (2021), *Training in Enterprises: New Evidence from 100 Case Studies*, Getting Skills Right, OECD Publishing, Paris, https://dx.doi.org/10.1787/7d63d210-en. [3]

OECD (2021), "What happened to jobs at high risk of automation?", OECD, Paris, http://www.oecd.org/future-of-work/reports-and-data/what-happened-to-jobs-at-high-risk-of-automation-2021.pdf. [10]

OECD (2020), *OECD Employment Outlook 2020: Worker Security and the COVID-19 Crisis*, OECD Publishing, Paris, https://dx.doi.org/10.1787/1686c758-en. [9]

OECD (2019), *OECD Employment Outlook 2019: The Future of Work*, OECD Publishing, Paris, https://dx.doi.org/10.1787/9ee00155-en. [2]

Osiander, C. and G. Stephan (2018), *Gerade geringqualifizierte Beschäftigte sehen bei der beruflichen Weiterbildung viele Hürden*, http://www.iab-forum.de/gerade-geringqualifizierte-beschaeftigte-sehen-bei-der-beruflichen-weiterbildung-viele-huerden. [16]

Zimmermann, K. et al. (2009), *NRW 2025: Vom Hort der alten Industrien zum Magnet der Moderne?*, IZA Standpunkte, No. 10. [13]

Notes

[1] • "**Dispositional barriers** refer to adults' attitudes, personality traits, perceptions and expectations around learning. Examples for this type of barrier include lack of interest, concerns about one's ability to succeed, having no hope of improving one's labour market chances, and the perception that one has learnt enough already or is too old to acquire new skills. Dispositional barriers can be grounded in innate personality traits as well as prior experiences with education and training that shaped the individual's view.

• **Situational barriers** pertain mostly to the personal and family situation of the individual. This includes their financial situation, existence of care responsibilities, lack of family or employer support and lack of time due to work commitments, among other factors.

• **Institutional barriers** relate to the availability, or lack thereof, of appropriate learning opportunities. This includes a lack of flexibility in the available provision concerning time and location, as well as a lack of relevant learning opportunities tailored to the specific learning needs (e.g. specific andragogic approaches) (OECD, 2021[4]).

[2] www.volkshochschule.de/kurswelt/arbeit_und_beruf/vhs-Bildungsberatung.php.

2 Low-qualified workers in Berlin and their career guidance options

Berlin's large service sector offers diverse employment opportunities and employs a workforce that is comparatively polarised by education. This creates particular challenges for the adult learning system and its support structures. Career guidance in Berlin is organised as a state-wide publicly funded network of private providers and is complemented by specialised offers, including advice for companies, to address these divergent needs. The chapter i) examines the labour market situation of low-qualified workers in Berlin; ii) gives an overview of the career guidance offers available to them; and iii) presents the characteristics of adults using career guidance as well as the main reasons for using these services.

Introduction

Over the past decade, Berlin has experienced a strong upswing in the labour market. The number of employed individuals increased almost 36% between 2010 and 2019 (cf. Germany: +20%). This upswing was largely driven by part-time workers, whose share rose from 24% to 34% as well as by immigration to Berlin from other parts of Germany and from abroad (IAB, 2021[1]).

The labour market in Berlin was more affected by the pandemic than the rest of Germany. A quarter of all workers worked in sectors that were severely affected by containment measures, notably tourism and leisure, hospitality (accommodation and catering) and culture and entertainment.

The extensive use of the German short-time work (STW) scheme has prevented mass lay-offs. In some manufacturing industries (electrical industry/ mechanical engineering, manufacturing of other goods) and automobile trade, however, STW is expected to turn into persistent employment declines, as these industries had already been experiencing below-average growth before the crisis. According to BiBB-IAB projections (IAB, 2021[2]), jobs will be lost primarily in manufacturing, but also in construction and in selected areas of the information and communication industry (publishing, audio-visual media and broadcasting and telecommunications).

Supporting workers in these industries through career guidance will be crucial to help them transition to jobs in high demand and to prevent surges in unemployment in the mid and long term. Low-qualified adults stand to profit the most from this support, as they require more advice on training and employment opportunities.

Infographic 2.1. Berlin's low-qualified adults

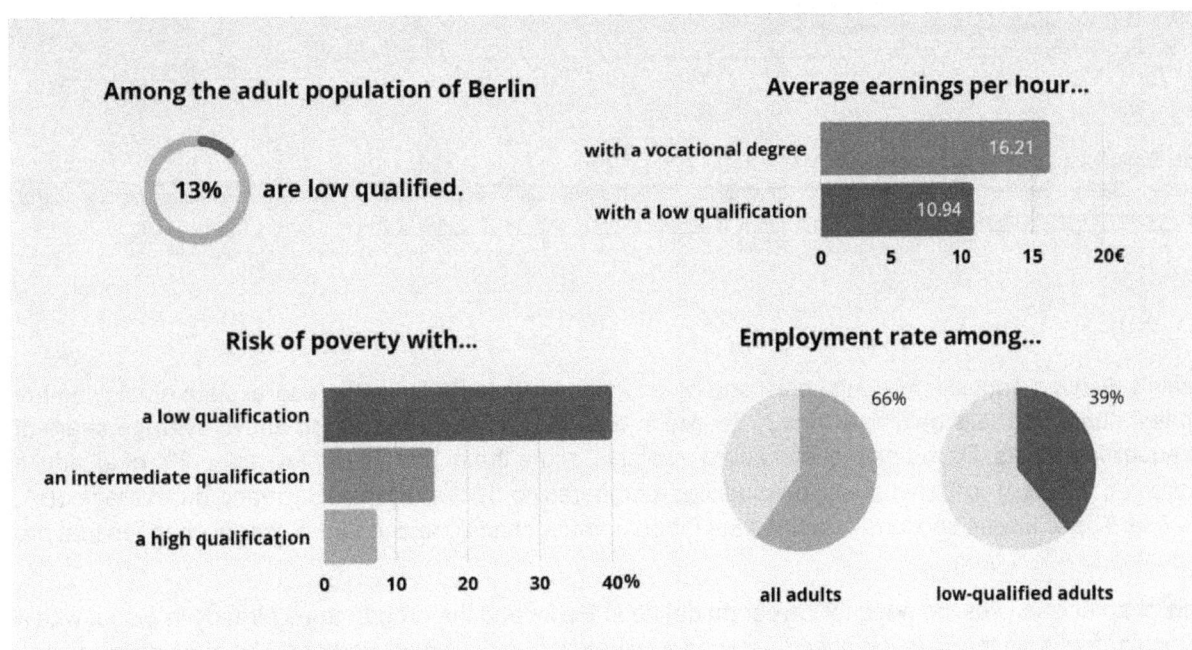

Among the adult population of Berlin

13% are low qualified.

Average earnings per hour...

with a vocational degree 16.21
with a low qualification 10.94

0   5   10   15   20€

Risk of poverty with...

a low qualification
an intermediate qualification
a high qualification

0   10   20   30   40%

Employment rate among...

66%   39%

all adults   low-qualified adults

Note: The share of low-qualified in the adult population refers to 2020. Employment rate and risk of poverty refers to 2019. Low qualification = ISCED 0-2, intermediate qualification = ISCED 3, 4, high qualification = ISCED 5,6. Average earnings refer to 2018.
Source: Eurostat (2020[3]), https://ec.europa.eu/eurostat/databrowser/view/edat_lfse_04/default/table?lang=en; Statistik Berlin Brandenburg (2018[4]), www.statistik-berlin-brandenburg.de/n-i-5-4j; Statistik Berlin Brandenburg (2019[5]), *Regionaler Sozialbericht Berlin Brandenburg 2019*, https://download.statistik-berlin-brandenburg.de/d0e9a12355b4b477/d60bd1c1cac8/AfS_Sozialbericht_2019_BBB.pdf; Berlin Senate Administration for Integration, Employment and Social Affairs (2019[6]).

Characteristics of career guidance users in Berlin

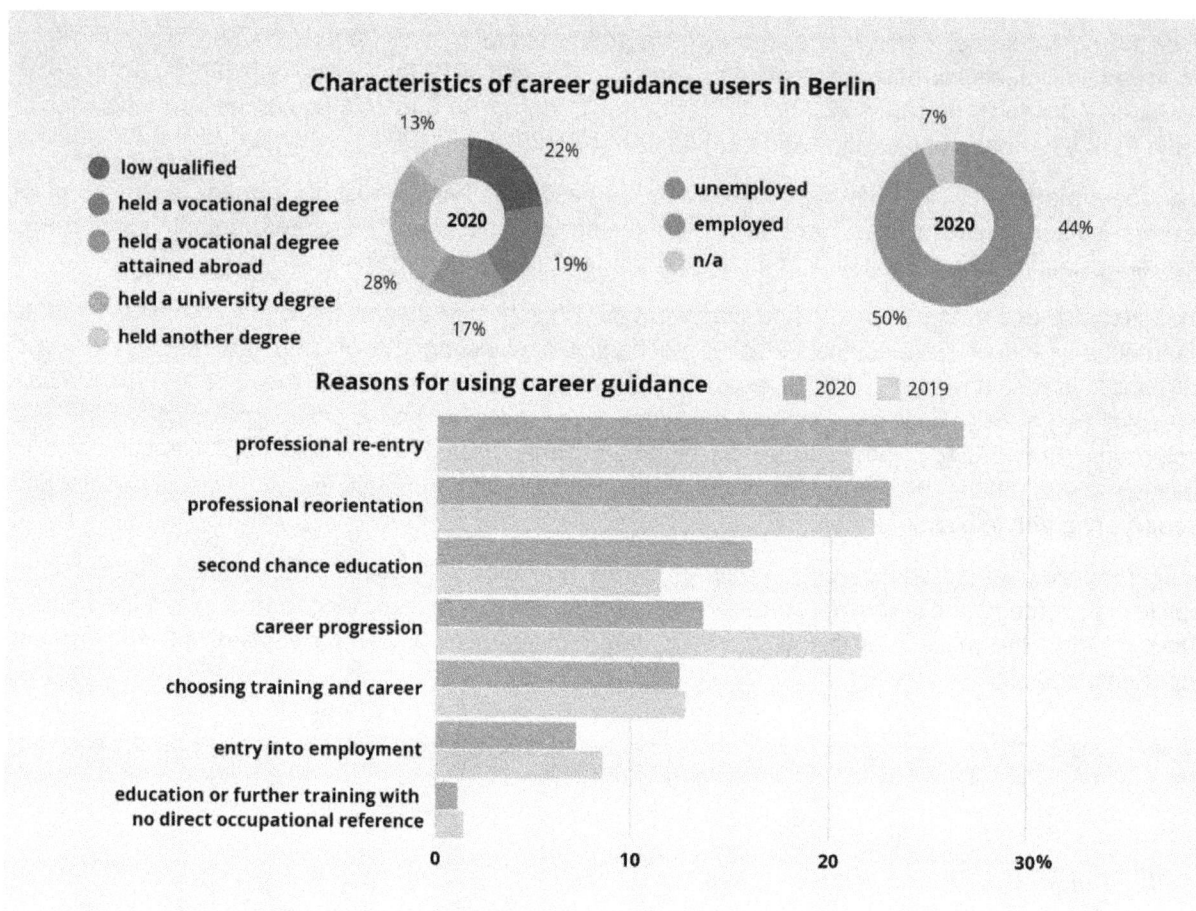

- low qualified
- held a vocational degree
- held a vocational degree attained abroad
- held a university degree
- held another degree

- unemployed
- employed
- n/a

2020: 13%, 22%, 19%, 17%, 28%

2020: 7%, 44%, 50%

Reasons for using career guidance ■ 2020 ■ 2019

- professional re-entry
- professional reorientation
- second chance education
- career progression
- choosing training and career
- entry into employment
- education or further training with no direct occupational reference

0   10   20   30%

Note: Some figures may not add up due to rounding.
Source: Berlin Senate Administration for Integration, Employment and Social Affairs (2019[6]), *Beratungs-Monitor 2019*, www.berlin.arbeitundleben.de/cms/upload/bildung_und_digitalisierung/Beratungs-Monitor_2019.pdf.

A picture of the low-qualified workers in Berlin

Berlin's working population is quite polarised by education. While Berlin is the federal state employing the highest share of adults holding a tertiary degree in Germany, it also employs an above average share of low-qualified adults. Based on the latest data available, more thatn 12% of employees[1] (13% of all adults (Eurostat, 2020[3])) in Berlin were low qualified compared to 10% (14%) in Germany on average (BA, 2020[7]). The following sections describe their labour market conditions and the structural changes that are expected to affect them.

This chapter analyses the need for career guidance in Berlin and the programmes already in place, with a particular focus on the situation of and services available for low-qualified workers. The main data sources used in this chapter are (i) the micro census conducted in 2018/19 by the federation and the federal states and (ii) the employment statistics of the BA from between 2018 and 2021, depending on the indicator. More details on the data can be found in Annex A.

Low qualifications are more common among men and migrants

Information on low-qualified adults provides a good approximation of the socio-demographic characteristics of individuals in this group. Composition is important to drive the nature of career guidance services and the channels through which career guidance is delivered. Among low-qualified adults in Berlin, there are slightly more men than women. Migrants are heavily over-represented among the low-qualified, making up more than half of the group (Statistik Berlin Brandenburg, 2019[8]).

Low employment rates and underemployment are common among low-qualified adults in Berlin, translating into low earnings and a high risk of poverty

Research shows that low-qualified adults have more limited labour market opportunities compared to those with a vocational degree (BIBB, 2021[9]) and are in addition disproportionally affected by structural and technological developments. In Berlin, only 39% of low-qualified adults (age 25 and above) are in employment (Statistik Berlin Brandenburg, 2019[10]), compared to 66% on average. This underscores the importance of supporting low-qualified employees to facilitate their transition to emerging sustainable employment opportunities.

Low-qualified employees in Berlin are also more likely to be underemployed: 38% work in part time employment compared to 33% on average in Berlin and 28% on average in Germany (Statistik Berlin Brandenburg, 2019[11]). Women and migrants are more likely to be employed part-time. In most cases, part-time employment, especially when involving few hours of work and low wages is involuntary and reflects difficulties in identifying opportunities for full-time work. Career guidance has the potential to support employees wanting to move out of under-employment.

Being low qualified also has a significant impact on earnings. The Structure of Earnings Survey, conducted every four years, found that in 2018 low-qualified employees earned an average of EUR 10.94 per hour in Berlin, while employees with a vocational qualification earned EUR 16.21 per hour (Statistik Berlin Brandenburg, 2018[4]). Similarly, qualification levels are closely related to the risk of poverty. In Berlin, 40% of low-qualified adults are at risk of poverty. With an intermediate degree (ISCED 3.4), the risk of poverty is 15%, similar to the German average (15%), while a high educational attainment reduces the risk of poverty to a below-average 7% (Statistik Berlin Brandenburg, 2019[5]). Supporting adults in reaching higher levels of qualification can significantly improve their financial situation.

Many low-qualified workers in Berlin need to transition out of industries hard hit by the pandemic and out of jobs at risk of automation

Most workers in Berlin work in the service sector (87%) (BA, 2021[12]), which has been hit hard by the COVID-19 pandemic. This is particularly the case for low-qualified adults who work mostly in retail, followed by social care jobs (excluding care homes), gastronomy, education and teaching, building maintenance and health care. Many of the low qualified working in the service sector are women (IAB, 2020[13]).

Low-qualified adults in Berlin mainly work in SMEs (61%). Recent evidence shows that employees in SMEs generally receive less career guidance and training on the job compared to those working for larger enterprises (OECD, 2021[14]). Germany and Berlin in particular, have initiatives in place to support SMEs in the provision of career guidance and training to their employees, which is an important step in the right direction.

Despite a good outlook in Berlin on average, a large share of low-qualified workers are in jobs at risk of automation for which demand is decreasing. Research by the IAB shows that the automation potential (*Substituierbarkeitspotenzial)* in Berlin is one of the lowest in Germany, with 15% of employees working in jobs with a high potential for automation.[2] This average hides significant variation. While automation potential is certainly low for Berlin's large share of high qualified adults working in non-routine high-skilled jobs (IAB, 2019[15]), low-qualified employees working in helper jobs – those requiring simple, less complex (routine) activities (Box 2.1) – are extremely vulnerable to automation. Figure 2.1 shows that in Berlin the automation potential among adults working in helper jobs is high at almost 50%, much higher than for adults working in expert or specialist jobs. Personalised career guidance could play a big role in supporting transitions to other sectors and occupations.

Figure 2.1. Automation potential in higher for low-qualified workers in Berlin

Automation potential by skills requirement level – Technological status 2016, employees subject to social security contributions as of 30 June 2017, percentage

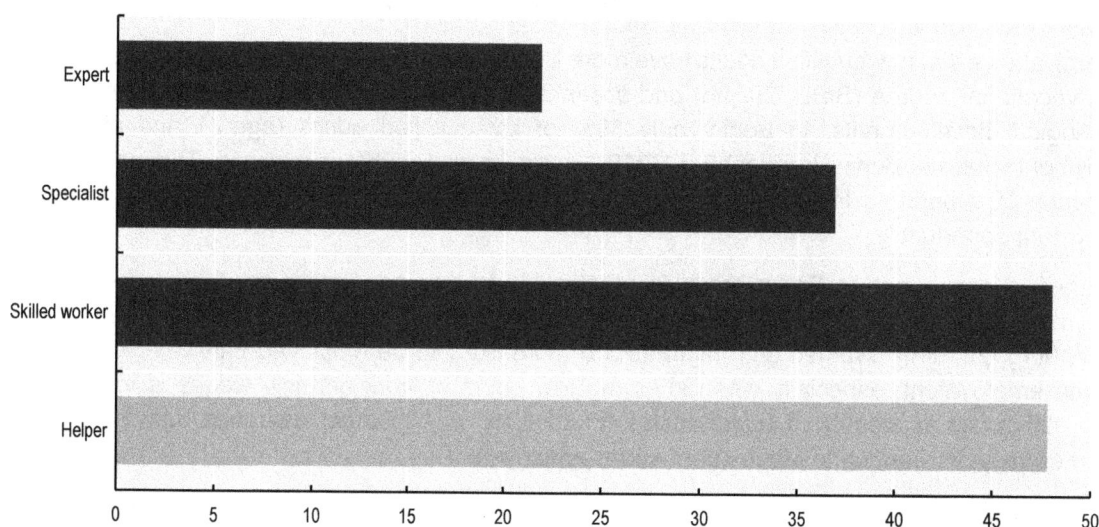

Note: The requirement level reflects the degree of complexity of the activity to be performed: Helper jobs involve assisting and semi-skilled activities (simple, less complex (routine) activities; usually no formal vocational qualification); Skilled jobs involve specialist-oriented activities (well-founded specialist knowledge and skills required; two to three years of vocational training); Specialist jobs involve complex specialist activities (special knowledge and skills, planning and management tasks, master craftsman or technician training, bachelor's degree); Expert jobs involve highly complex activities (expert knowledge, performance and management tasks, at least four years of higher education).
Source: IAB (2019[15]), *IAB-Regional Berlin-Brandenburg 2|2019 – Mögliche Auswirkungen der Digitalisierung in Berlin und Brandenburg*, http://doku.iab.de/regional/BB/2019/regional_bb_0219.pdf.

Box 2.1. Job categories often used in German statistics

In German statistics, jobs are divided into four categories reflecting the degree of complexity of the activity to be performed:

- **Helper** jobs involve assisting and semi-skilled activities (simple, less complex (routine) activities; usually no formal vocational qualification);
- **Skilled** jobs involve specialist-oriented activities (well-founded specialist knowledge and skills required; two to three years of vocational training);
- **Specialist** jobs involve complex specialist activities (special knowledge and skills, planning and management tasks, master craftsman or technician training, bachelor's degree);
- **Expert** jobs involve highly complex activities (expert knowledge, performance and management tasks, at least four years of higher education).

Source: BA (2019[16]), *Begriffserläuterungen „Berufe auf einen Blick"*, https://statistik.arbeitsagentur.de/DE/Statischer-Content/Statistiken/Interaktive-Angebote/Berufe-auf-einen-Blick/Generische-Publikationen/Berufe-auf-einen-Blick-Begriffserlaeuterungen.pdf.

Although the risk of automation for employees in skilled jobs – requiring 2-3 years of vocational training – is approximately the same as for helper jobs, the demand in skilled jobs is still significantly higher and growing faster compared to the demand in helper jobs in Berlin (BA, 2019[17]). Over recent years (2014-18), twice as many additional skilled jobs[3] were created in Berlin compared to helper jobs. Looking at the different occupations, labour supply exceeds demand strongly in transport, logistics, protection and security (12 unemployed per vacancy), the second most held occupations by low-qualified adults (BA, 2021[18]).

Job vacancy statistics[4] confirm a decline in openings for helper jobs in Germany. Among all job offers posted online, the share of helper jobs has declined over the past years and particularly during the COVID-19 crisis (IMF, 2020[19]; OECD, 2021[20]; OECD, 2021[21]). While it is true that most job offers for helper jobs are not posted online, the available data support the trend of a declining growth in the demand for low-qualified labour.

Career guidance offers in Berlin

This section looks at the structures put in place to guide adults through the changing world of work. While, as stated above, no career guidance designed specifically for low-qualified workers exists in Germany, the offers listed below are open to all adults and are complemented by services that are particularly relevant for low-qualified workers. In addition, employers have access to support in planning their skills needs, provide career guidance and in investing in training for their employees.

As mentioned before, the career guidance offers in Berlin are organised in a core network called Guidance on Education and Profession (*Berliner Beratung zu Bildung und Beruf*, BBB). It is complemented by the BA's LBBiE, the VHS programmes and programmes organised through the IQ-Network and the guidance network Career Progression for Women (Table 2.1). A centralised platform provides information and contact details of all BBB locations, as well as of those institutions and networks they co-operate with. So far, career guidance offers by social partners are excluded, but may be included in the future.

Table 2.1. Career guidance networks in Berlin

Original name	English name	Actors involved (incl. funders)	Target group
Berliner Beratung zu Bildung und Beruf, BBB	Berlin Guidance on Education and Profession network	Senate Department for Integration, Labour and Social Affairs, SenIAS	All individuals
Fachberatung berufliche Qualifizierung, FbQu	Vocational qualification counselling	SANQ e. V.	Individuals seeking a formal diploma via partial qualifications
Erfolg mit Sprache und Abschluss, EMSA	Success with language and qualification	Arbeit und Bildung e. V.	Migrants
Qualifizierungsberatung in KMU	Qualification guidance for SMEs	GesBiT mbH	SMEs
Mobile Beratung zu Bildung und Beruf für geflüchtete Menschen, MoBiBe	Mobile counselling on education and careers for refugees	KOBRA (Berliner Frauenbund 1945 e.V.), Senate Department for Health, Care and Equality	Refugees
Lebensbegleitende Berufsberatung im Erwerbsleben, LBBiE	Lifelong Vocational Guidance for adults in employment	BA	All individuals
Volkshochschulen, VHS	Network of adult education centres	VHS	All individuals
IQ-Netzwerk	IQ-Network	BMAS, ESF, BAMF, BMBF, BA	Migrants
Berufsperspektiven für Frauen	Guidance network Career Progression for Women	Senate Department for Health, Care and Equality	Women
Grund-Bildungs-Zentrum Berlin, GBZ	Centre for Basic Education	Senate Department for Integration, Labour and Social Affairs, VHS	Adults with low literacy

Source: BMAS (2021[22]), Das *Bundesprogramm „Aufbau von Weiterbildungsverbünden" – Übersicht zu den geförderten Projekten*, www.bmas.de/SharedDocs/Downloads/DE/Aus-Weiterbildung/budnesprogramm-aufbau-von-weiterbildungsverbuenden-uebersicht-projekte.pdf;jsessionid=2F26CCDA4749511239DA40087A2E12D9.delivery2-master?__blob=publicationFile&v=2.

The Berlin Guidance on Education and Profession network brings together most of the career guidance programmes available in the federal state

In Berlin, the Berlin Senate Department for Integration, Labour and Social Affairs, SenIAS, has set up the network Educational Counselling and Career Guidance in Berlin (*Berliner Beratung zu Bildung und Beruf*, BBB). The core network consists of ten counselling centres, seven of which provide **general** educational and job related career guidance and three provide **specialised** support. Specialised centres focus on professional post-qualification (*Fachberatung berufliche Qualifizierung*, FbQu), on language related career guidance needs (*Erfolg mit Sprache und Abschluss, EMSA*) and on support for SMEs (*Qualifizierungsberatung in KMU*). These centres are distributed across the federal state so that almost every district (*Bezirk*) hosts one of them. Since 2016, the centres are complemented by specialised mobile counselling on education and careers for refugees (*Mobile Beratung zu Bildung und Beruf für geflüchtete Menschen*, MoBiBe), responding to the challenges Berlin is facing in integrating refugees.

BBB career guidance does not specifically target low-qualified adults but includes services that are particular relevant for this target group, including counselling on:

- CET.
- Vocational (re-)orientation and CV.
- Career prospects and access to employment (career path, career development, application strategy, etc.).
- Employment and qualification (job situation, in-company qualification, career development and flexibility).
- Learning, forms of learning and learning strategies.
- Funding and financing.

All centres carry out a mapping of competences and qualifications, provide computers and internet for (supervised) personal research in CET databases and to prepare application documents, and organise workshops on topics related to applying for jobs, starting a career, returning to work, or learning to learn. Additional services include the assessment of (German) language levels, advice on language courses and the use of the "Infotelefon Weiterbildung" of the BMBF. Berlin is one of the federal states that regulate education and training leave, which BBB also provides guidance on.[5]

The centres are selected by the SenIAS via a call for tenders and are fully publicly financed. In 2020, a new call for tenders led to the selection of several new career guidance providers and the closing of the popular learning shops (*Lernläden*). However, the new providers offer similar career guidance services as the learning shops used to provide. A concept paper (*Fachkonzept*) written by the SenIAS sets principles on the provision of career guidance by the centres:

- Provision must be free of charge to the individuals and SMEs.
- The use of career guidance is voluntary.
- Career guidance must be offered in several languages.
- Provision must be available city-wide and reachable by public transport.
- Career guidance services have to be independent of own interests. While the centres often offer in-house adult learning opportunities, they must advertise the services in the best interest of the individual or SME.

The providers are private companies, associations, non-profit organisations that generally develop, advise and implement socially oriented projects in the areas of labour market and employment, lifelong learning, and the promotion of democracy and integration at federal, state and municipal level.

The concept paper also contains common quality standards and the Quality Framework Berlin Model (*Qualitätsrahmen Berliner Modell,* QBM), to ensure equivalent or comparable quality of the career guidance centres in Berlin. The QBM defines a procedure of recognition and certification of guidance providers in the network, based on the Quality Concept for Guidance (*Qualitätskonzept für Beratung*) by k.o.s GmbH. It serves to ensure and improve the quality of guidance, which is then validated through an external quality assurance procedure. The guidance providers are awarded a quality seal and accredited according to this procedure every 3 years since 2014. The Quality Co-ordination Office (*Koordinierungsstelle Qualität*), run by k.o.s GmbH, moderates and accompanies the BBB on topics such as quality assurance and certification and professionalisation as well as public relations.

In addition, the Quality Co-ordination Office supports providers to foster innovation, modernisation efforts and structural changes via its project "learned further" (*weiter gelernt*) that focusses specifically on the topics digitalisation, methodology and didactics, competence development, quality management, personnel and organisational development. The concrete services range from workshops, seminars, webinars and advisory services to studies and networking.

The SenIAS runs an online platform[6] for the network under the same name, which presents the ten centres, describes their services and provides contact details. As seven of the centres provide general guidance, individuals do not need any prior knowledge on their exact needs, but they can find out together during the guidance process. Users are also invited to browse CET offers through a dedicated search engine and database. In addition to the BBB core network, the online platform also provides links to other actors in the career guidance landscape as part of a broader co-operation network. The BA, for example, has recently added their offers (see Box 2.2) in the area of career guidance (*Lebensbegleitende Berufsberatung im Erwerbsleben, LBBiE der Arbeitsagenturen*). The VHS, the IQ-Network and the guidance network Career Progression for Women (*Berufsperspektiven für Frauen*) also offer their expertise on the platform. The vision of the SenIAS and the BA is to have all existing career guidance offers in Berlin included on the website. This would also include offers by business associations, chambers of commerce, guilds, etc.

On the platform, individuals are put in contact with career guidance providers and the latter can redirect them to specialised training providers as well as to district counselling centres, basic education centres and the other actors mentioned above. As such, the access to career guidance services requires no prior knowledge on existing offers from the individual or SME. Behind the scenes, the SenIAS is responsible for the overall co-ordination.

In addition to co-operation with other career guidance providers, BBB centres also work closely with other social services aiming at providing integrated services to the extent possible. For example, debt counsellors are located directly in some of the centres and close relations are established with integration services and social inclusion counselling centres.

The BBB network also runs outreach activities, with a new one recently established specifically for immigrants. General outreach activities have always existed organised by the career guidance centres in co-operation with local associations, neighbourhood houses[7] (*Nachbarschaftshäuser*), neighbourhood management[8] (*Quartiersmanagement*), women's shelters and cafés (*Frauenhäuser, -cafés*).

Box 2.2. Integration of LBBiE in Berlin

The BA's new programme Lifelong Vocational Guidance (*Lebensbegleitende Berufsberatung*, LBB) aims to shift the BA's approach, previously oriented towards ensuring employability in the short term, to a more proactive approach of supporting individuals in career planning and decision-making over the life-course. Its career guidance strand aimed at adults in employment (*Lebensbegleitende Berufsberatung im Erwerbsleben,* LBBiE) is still in the development phase by the Berlin BA offices. BA and SenIAS co-ordinate the integration of their services in regular meetings and close consultation.

While the division of responsibilities is not clear-cut, each of the two actors has developed specialised competencies that complement the other's expertise. The most significant difference is the general direction of career guidance services: while the BA's career guidance services are meant to facilitate matching labour demand with supply, SenIAS's counsellors are more focused on assessing individual interests, competencies and aspirations to match them with available training and employment opportunities. As such, the services provided by SenIAS centres are better suited to working adults. SenIAS centres are also used by adults who are generally interested in CET but may need support in identifying their personal needs and available options. As a result, SenIAS centres are better placed to provide broader career guidance and then refer clients to the BA's or other actors' services, as appropriate.

The BBB network is complemented by other specialised ones

Several other networks play an important role in the career guidance landscape in Berlin and complement the BBB in several ways. Most of the networks are well organised and align the offers of their members on a regular basis.

One network that is mainly known for the provision of adult learning, but which also provides career guidance to adults is the **network of adult education centres** (*Volkshochschulen*, VHS). The network links the different VHS sites in Berlin which are otherwise independent providers mostly financed by the districts and participants' contributions. The VHS in Berlin offer more German language courses compared to other federal states in Germany (OECD, forthcoming[23]), which puts them in a good position to offer career guidance to adults with a migrant background through the contacts that have already been established. MoBiBe, the specialised mobile counselling for refugees, is also located at the VHS facilities.

As described in Chapter 1, another network that operates nationwide, including in Berlin is the **IQ-Network**. Its central field of action is the recognition of qualifications acquired abroad and the provision of career guidance related to the recognition process. Different initiatives provide counselling services and help migrants find work that matches their qualifications – regardless of the outcome of the recognition procedure. One of the main factors of success of the network is the strong co-operation with other labour market and adult learning institutions in Berlin.

The guidance **network Career prospects for women** (*Berufsperspektiven für Frauen*) offers free counselling for women through eight projects at eight locations in Berlin on CET. Some of the eight locations offer general career guidance while others specialise in specific topics such as CET, or transitions into the labour market. The network runs a counselling phone line for migrant women free of charge and in several languages and also offers workshops, discussion groups and computer workstations. It is funded by the Senate Department for Health, Care and Equality, Department of Women and Equality in Berlin.

Finally, the Berlin's Centre for Basic Education (*Grund-Bildungs-Zentrum Berlin,* GBZ) offers information and awareness raising initiatives, counselling and networking on adult literacy and basic education topics for individuals, course instructors, multipliers, employees in institutions and companies, decision-makers from politics and society, and media representatives (Berliner Grund-Bildungs-Zentrum, 2021[24]). It is funded by the Senate Department for Integration, Labour and Social Affairs, and works in close co-operation with the VHS. They are currently piloting a concept of mobile counselling.

Advice on CET for companies to encourage the skill development of employees

Experts report the particular difficulty in reaching low-qualified employees via the available career guidance services, agreeing that more personalised guidance via coaches, colleagues and supervisors, especially in, or in co-operation with, companies, would be the best channel to reach this group. However, support services that help enterprises to assess their skills needs, provide career guidance at work and invest in training for their employees would be needed to build capacity among enterprises, particularly SMEs, and to ensure that services benefit low-qualified workers (OECD, 2021[14]).

As described above, one of the BBB counselling centres specialises on support for SMEs (*Qualifizierungsberatung in KMU*). The centre is currently hosted by the GesBiT mbH, a company running socially oriented projects. Thanks to the funding by Berlin's Senate Department for Integration, Labour and Social Affairs, all services for SMEs are free of charge and available via various channels. They include counselling on analysing training needs and strategies, on implementing company training goals, on qualifications for employees, on CET funding opportunities and their conditions as well as awareness raising for companies regarding training for low-qualified and older employees and occupational health management.

As in most federal states, the Chamber of Commerce and Industry also offers guidance for companies in Berlin via similar services as the ones listed above. It also offers counselling on other activities aiming at attracting and retaining skilled workers such as organising internships or hiring foreign workers.

Berlin was also one of the first federal states to set up a CET network supported by the BMAS's federal programme. The networks focus on supporting employers in specific sectors or regions. Among the 39 chosen networks, four will be established in Berlin (Table 2.2). The interest in the creation of networks was strong, which underscores the need for better co-operation and for structured communication channels among actors in the CET landscape.

Table 2.2. CET networks under the federal programme in Berlin

Original name	English name	Actors involved	Focus
Modellhafte Etablierung einer Koordinierungs-stelle für den Aufbau eines Weiterbildungsverbundes im Automotive-Cluster Berlin-Brandenburg (MEKA-BB)	Pilot co-ordination office for the development of a CET network in the automotive cluster Berlin-Brandenburg	Association for Vocational Education Research e.V. (IBBF); Society for the Promotion of Educational Research and Qualification GmbH (GEBIFO); Centre for vocational and continuous education GmbH Ludwigsfelde-Luckenwalde	Automotive
HOGA.Co	HOGA.Co	bildungsmarkt e.v., Dehoga, Food and Catering Trade Union NGG, IHK	Hospitality
R-Learning Kollektiv	R-Learning Collective	GFBM Akademie gGmbH; ITS mobility GmbH; ABB VET centre Berlin; Berufsbildungsverein Prenzlau	Control technology, digitalisation and automation
Weiterbildungsverbund der Berlin-Brandenburger Unternehmensnetzwerke	CET network of the enterprises in Berlin-Brandenburg	TeachCom Edutainment gGmbH	Digitalisation, sustainability, artificial intelligence, quality of training and intercultural organisational development

Note: Since all networks are approved but most are still being implemented, information on specific foci may not always be available.

Use of career guidance in Berlin

The BBB network is relatively successful in reaching low-qualified adults, as more than a quarter of the users do not hold a vocational education degree. However, a large share of users are unemployed (39%, down from 55% in 2019), resulting in a duplication of services also provided by the public employment service. As the rationale behind career guidance services is shifting from supporting the unemployed to facilitating labour market transitions, there is a clear opportunity for the network to set a stronger focus on providing career guidance to low-qualified workers.

The data on career guidance in Berlin used in this section cover the services offered by the core BBB network only, including the general BBB programme, the mobile counselling for refugees MoBiBe, the post-qualification guidance FbQu and the service for language related guidance needs EMSA.

Career guidance use declined among low-qualified adults in the pandemic

The yearly Guidance Monitor (*Beratungs-Monitor*) includes data and analysis collected within the BBB network in five areas: (i) demand for career guidance and available services; (ii) data on the socio-demographic characteristics of users; (iii) the reasons for seeking career guidance and the content of the guidance sessions; (iv) the outcomes and consequences of the guidance processes and (v) access to guidance services. The latest available data refer to the year 2020. The data show strong differences compared to the pre-pandemic use in 2019, which is why this section includes some comparisons between the two years.

In 2020 counsellors in Berlin held 20 128 **counselling sessions** with 12 347 **individuals**, down from 2019 where the figures were 22 438 and 15 886, respectively. The majority of the sessions took place in the context of the general BBB programme (61%) and the remaining ones as part of the specialised programmes: MoBiBe (37%) and FbQu (1%) and EMSA (1%).

Users of the general BBB programme were mostly female (62%) and aged between 35 and 44 years old. Almost half (45%) had a migration background. Twenty-two percent of users did not hold any vocational education degree (2019: 26%), almost twice the share of low-qualified adults in Berlin's population (12%). In 2019 they constituted the highest share among all users, but the pandemic seems to have shifted the majority of users towards adults holding a university degree in 2020 (28%, up from 22% in 2019).

Almost 26% of BBB users were in full-time employment and 16% were employed part-time (including the German concept of mini-jobs). While 37% of the users were still looking for a new job (Figure 2.2).

Figure 2.2. More workers used career guidance during the pandemic

Career guidance users by employment status, 2019, 2020, percentage

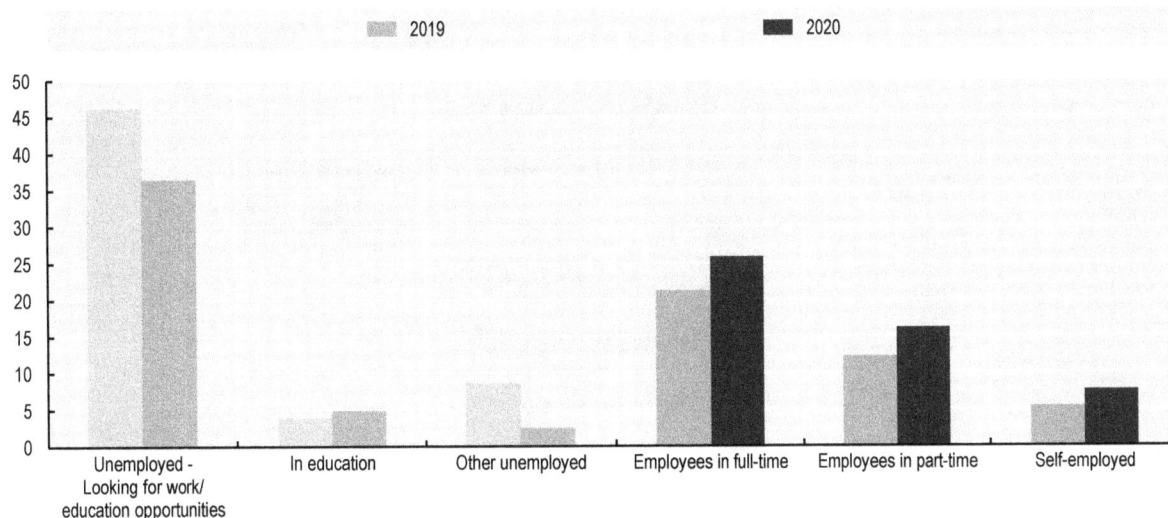

Source: Berlin Senate Administration for Integration, Employment and Social Affairs (2019[6]), *Beratungs-Monitor 2019*, www.berlin.arbeitundleben.de/cms/upload/bildung_und_digitalisierung/Beratungs-Monitor_2019.pdf.

In comparison, the users of MoBiBe were primarily male (55%, down from 58% in 2019) and younger than BBB users. Most of them come from Syria, followed by Iran and Afghanistan. In total, almost 73% (up from 66% in 2019) had a school-leaving certificate and 41% held a technical vocational or university degree compared to 34% in 2019.

The most common channel through which adults in Berlin heard about the possibility to use career guidance is their personal environment. In 2020, 23% relied on their friends, family and colleagues. Jobcentres (BA agencies for longer-term unemployed and those in precarious employment) were the second most common channel (18%) in 2019 but were cited less often in 2020 (11%). Instead more adults stated that they already knew about guidance possibilities (16%) and 14% found the information via their own research. Public advertisement campaigns seem to have been less useful in raising awareness of career guidance services, with the exception of refugees using the MoBiBe guidance programme, where 17% reported hearing of the services from a public campaign.

The pandemic has contributed to a shift in career guidance services from supporting job search to facilitating sustainable labour market transitions

As mentioned above, the pandemic seems to have shifted the focus of career guidance from job intermediation to supporting sustainable transitions to emerging occupations. Sixty-five percent of the users of career guidance services now seek support with career development, (re-)orientation on the labour market and information on further training.

Figure 2.3. The demand for guidance on career development increased during the pandemic

Career guidance users by reasons for using guidance, 2019, 2020, percentage

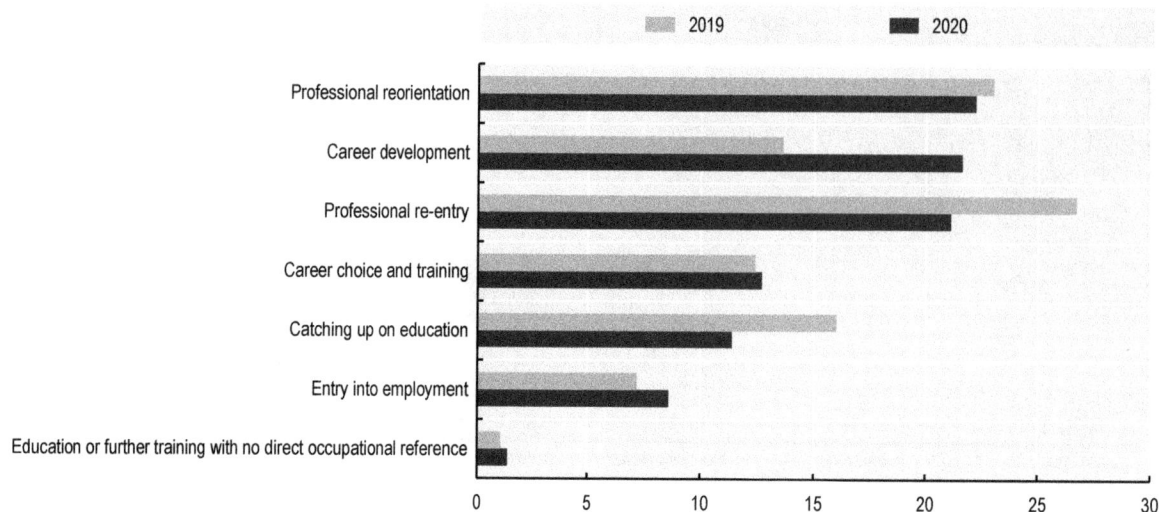

Source: Berlin Senate Administration for Integration, Employment and Social Affairs (2019[6]), *Beratungs-Monitor 2019*, www.berlin.arbeitundleben.de/cms/upload/bildung_und_digitalisierung/Beratungs-Monitor_2019.pdf.

References

BA (2021), *Arbeitsmarktreport NRW 2021*, https://statistik.arbeitsagentur.de/SiteGlobals/Forms/Suche/Einzelheftsuche_Formular.html?to pic_f=amr-amr&r_f=bl_Nordrhein-Westfalen. [18]

BA (2021), *Beschäftigung nach Wirtschaftszweigen (WZ 2008) - hochgerechnete Werte*, https://statistik.arbeitsagentur.de/Statistikdaten/Detail/202105/iiia6/beschaeftigung-sozbe-monatsheft-wz/monatsheft-wz-d-0-202105-pdf.pdf?__blob=publicationFile&v=1. [12]

BA (2020), *Qualifikationsspezifische Arbeitslosenquoten (Jahreszahlen)*, https://statistik.arbeitsagentur.de/SiteGlobals/Forms/Suche/Einzelheftsuche_Formular.html?n n=1610088&topic_f=alo-qualiquote. [7]

BA (2019), *Arbeitsmarkttelegramm Berlin*. [17]

BA (2019), *Begriffserläuterungen „Berufe auf einen Blick"*, https://statistik.arbeitsagentur.de/DE/Statischer-Content/Statistiken/Interaktive-Angebote/Berufe-auf-einen-Blick/Generische-Publikationen/Berufe-auf-einen-Blick-Begriffserlaeuterungen.pdf?__blob=publicationFile&v=6. [16]

Berliner Grund-Bildungs-Zentrum (2021), *Berliner Grund-Bildungs-Zentrum*, https://grundbildung-berlin.de/kurz-info. [24]

BIBB (2021), *Datenreport zum Berufsbildungsbericht 2021*, http://www.bibb.de/dokumente/pdf/bibb-datenreport-2021.pdf. [9]

BMAS (2021), *Das Bundesprogramm "Aufbau von Weiterbildungsverbünden" - Übersicht zu den geförderten Projekten*, http://www.bmas.de/DE/Arbeit/Aus-und-Weiterbildung/Weiterbildungsrepublik/Weiterbildungsverbuende/weiterbildungsverbuende-art.html. [22]

Eurostat (2020), *Population by educational attainment level, sex and NUTS 2 regions*, https://ec.europa.eu/eurostat/databrowser/view/edat_lfse_04/default/table?lang=en. [3]

IAB (2021), *Arbeitsmarkt in Berlin-Brandenburg: Coronabedingter Beschäftigungseinbruch nach langjährigem Wachstum*, http://doku.iab.de/regional/BB/2021/regional_bb_0221.pdf. [1]

IAB (2021), *IAB-Kurzbericht: Demografie und Strukturwandel prägen weiterhin die regionale Entwicklung der Arbeitsmärkte*, http://doku.iab.de/kurzber/2021/kb2021-01.pdf. [2]

IAB (2020), *IAB-Forschungsbericht 16*, http://doku.iab.de/forschungsbericht/2020/fb1620.pdf. [13]

IAB (2019), *IAB-Regional Berlin-Brandenburg 2|2019 - Mögliche Auswirkungen der Digitalisierung in Berlin und Brandenburg*, http://doku.iab.de/regional/BB/2019/regional_bb_0219.pdf. [15]

IMF (2020), *Disparities in real time - Online job posting analysis shows the extent of the pandemic's damage, especially to women and youth*, http://www.imf.org/external/pubs/ft/fandd/2020/12/value-of-real-time-data-in-covid-crisis-chen.htm. [19]

OECD (2021), "An assessment of the impact of COVID-19 on job and skills demand using online job vacancy data", *OECD Policy Responses to Coronavirus (COVID-19)*, OECD Publishing, Paris, https://dx.doi.org/10.1787/20fff09e-en. [21]

OECD (2021), *OECD Employment Outlook 2021: Navigating the COVID-19 Crisis and Recovery*, OECD Publishing, Paris, https://dx.doi.org/10.1787/5a700c4b-en. [20]

OECD (2021), *Training in Enterprises: New Evidence from 100 Case Studies*, Getting Skills Right, OECD Publishing, Paris, https://dx.doi.org/10.1787/7d63d210-en. [14]

OECD (forthcoming), *Future-Proofing Adult Learning in Berlin*, OECD Reviews on Local Job Creation, OECD Publishing, Paris. [23]

Senatsverwaltung für Integration, Arbeit und Soziales (2019), *Beratungs-Monitor 2019*, http://www.berlin.arbeitundleben.de/cms/upload/bildung_und_digitalisierung/Beratungs-Monitor_2019.pdf. [6]

Statistik Berlin Brandenburg (2019), *Bevölkerung im Alter von 25 und mehr Jahren, darunter mit niedrigem Bildungsstand, darunter erwerbstätig*. [10]

Statistik Berlin Brandenburg (2019), *Microcensus data 2019*, https://www.statistikportal.de/de/sbe/ergebnisse/qualifikationsniveau/personen-mit-niedrigem-bildungsstand. [11]

Statistik Berlin Brandenburg (2019), *Mikrozensus*, http://www.statistik-berlin-brandenburg.de/bevoelkerung/demografie/mikrozensus. [8]

Statistik Berlin Brandenburg (2019), *Regionaler Sozialbericht Berlin Brandenburg 2019*. [5]

Statistik Berlin Brandenburg (2018), *Verdienststrukturerhebung*, http://www.statistik-berlin-brandenburg.de/n-i-5-4j. [4]

Notes

1 Employees subject to compulsory social insurance (Sozialversicherungspflichtig Beschäftigte).

2 Automation potential (Substituierungspotenzial) = Proportion of activities that could potentially be done by computers or computer-controlled machines already today. It is divided in high potential (100-70%), medium potential (70-30%) and low potential (30-0%).

3 Skilled workers (*Fachkräfte*) perform professionally oriented activities. As a rule, at least two years of vocational training or comparable competences are required to perform these activities.

4 Burning glass data: Burning Glass Technologies (BGT) is an analytics software company that collects, scrapes and analyses job postings from thousands of online sources and job portals. BGT uses text mining to extract and code information from each job description such as experience, qualifications, and skills that employers are seeking. BGT then removes duplicate postings across sites and assigns attributes including geographic locations, required educational qualifications, and industry. BGT data allow for tracking of job vacancy postings, which reflect hiring dynamics, and skills demand at disaggregated level by geography and by detailed occupation and industry.

5 In Berlin, leave exists since 1990 and individuals who have worked for at least 6 months in a company are entitled to 10 days per 2 years for over 25-year-old adults and 10 days per year for adults below 25 years old. During the leave, employers are obliged to continue paying the individual's salary. In few of them, such as Rhineland-Palatine, employers can request government support to cover part of these costs. Direct costs of CET participation are not covered by education and training leave regulation.

6 https://beratung-bildung-beruf.berlin.

7 Civic initiatives to incentivise interaction between different population groups in a neighbourhood.

8 It is a state provision for the social stabilisation of urban districts. Its aim is to play a mediating role between the neighbourhood and the administration (vertical) and between existing neighbourhood institutions (horizontal).

3 Low-qualified workers in North Rhine-Westphalia and their career guidance options

NRW's share of low-qualified adults is comparatively high and while most of them are in employment, many are struggling with low job quality. The state-wide publicly funded career guidance network of private providers is open to workers and unemployed adults. Additional specialised services target vulnerable population groups such as those affected by the substantive structural changes in NRW or individuals with a migration background. The chapter i) examines the labour market situation of low-qualified workers in NRW; ii) gives an overview of the career guidance offers available to them; and iii) presents the characteristics of adults using career guidance as well as the main reasons for using these services.

Introduction

As the most populated federal state in Germany, North Rhine-Westphalia (NRW) is highly diverse in terms of local labour market performance. The city in Germany with the highest unemployment rate at 15% is in NRW while other cities have among the lowest rates, close to 3%. NRW's labour market is also diverse in terms of the sectoral composition of employment. The economy is still shaped by the dominant energy and manufacturing (*Verarbeitendes Gewerbe*) industries (DIE, 2019[1]). However, environmental and societal pressures are increasingly threatening these sectors, leading to changes in skill demand. In parallel, the service sector has been expanding to employ in total almost 74% of the workers in 2021.

NRW's labour market is slowly recovering from the COVID-19 crisis and for some population groups the recovery is particularly difficult. While many labour market indicators are approaching pre-crisis levels for the general population, the latest available figures on unemployment among low-qualified adults and long-term-unemployed remain above pre-crisis levels. As it is the case in Berlin, helper jobs generally held by low-qualified adults are still affected by the aftermath of the COVID-19 pandemic.

As described previously, workers without or with low qualifications are particularly vulnerable to changes like those affecting NRW. The provision of career guidance and advice would be crucial to support their retraining and job search.

Infographic 3.1. NRW's low-qualified adults

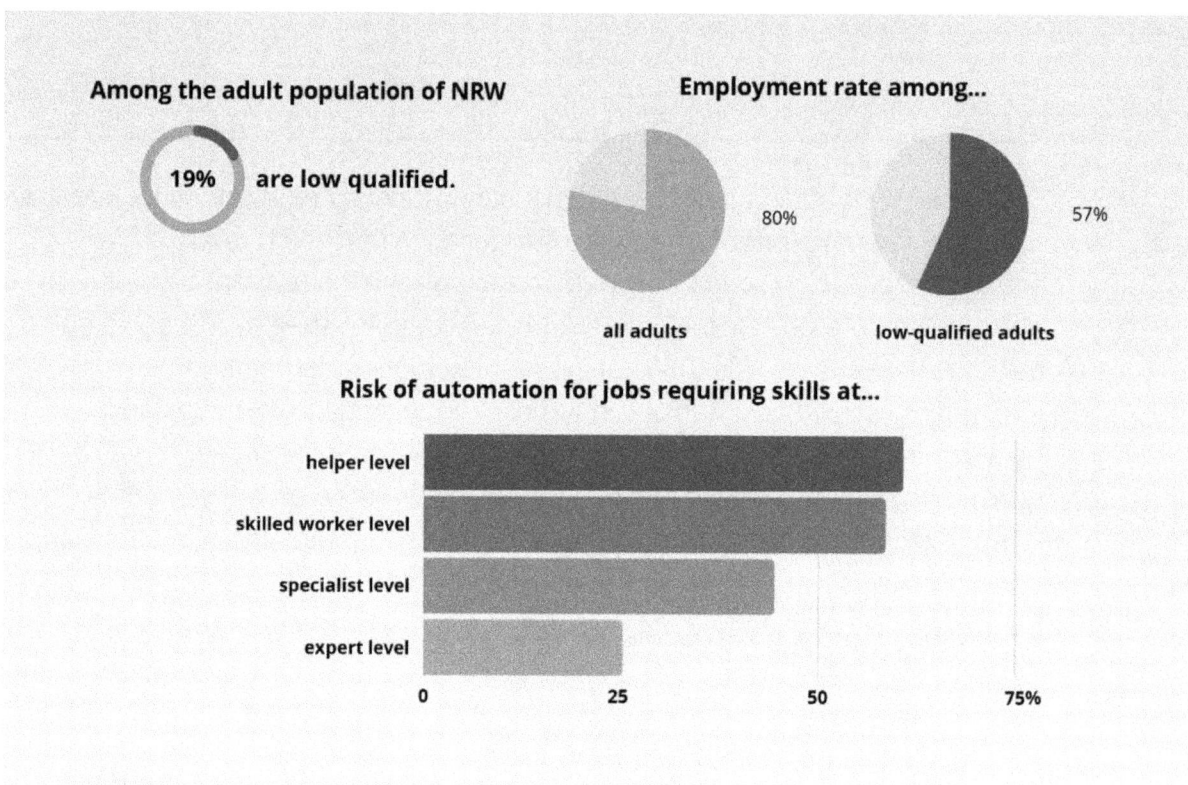

Among the adult population of NRW

19% are low qualified.

Employment rate among...

80%

all adults

57%

low-qualified adults

Risk of automation for jobs requiring skills at...

helper level	
skilled worker level	
specialist level	
expert level	

0   25   50   75%

Note: The share of low-qualified in the adult population refers to 2020. Employment rate refers to 2018. Potential for automation refers to 2019, the use of career guidance indicators refer to 2020.
Source: Eurostat (2020[2]), https://ec.europa.eu/eurostat/databrowser/view/edat_lfse_04/default/table?lang=en; MAGS (2020[3]), *Sozialbericht NRW 2020*, www.sozialberichte.nrw.de/sozialberichterstattung_nrw/aktuelle_berichte/SB2020.pdf; IAB (2019[4]), *Substituierbarkeitspotenziale in Nordrhein-Westfalen 2019 – Ausgewählte Ergebnisse*; G.I.B. (2021[5]).

Infographic 3.2. Career guidance use in NRW

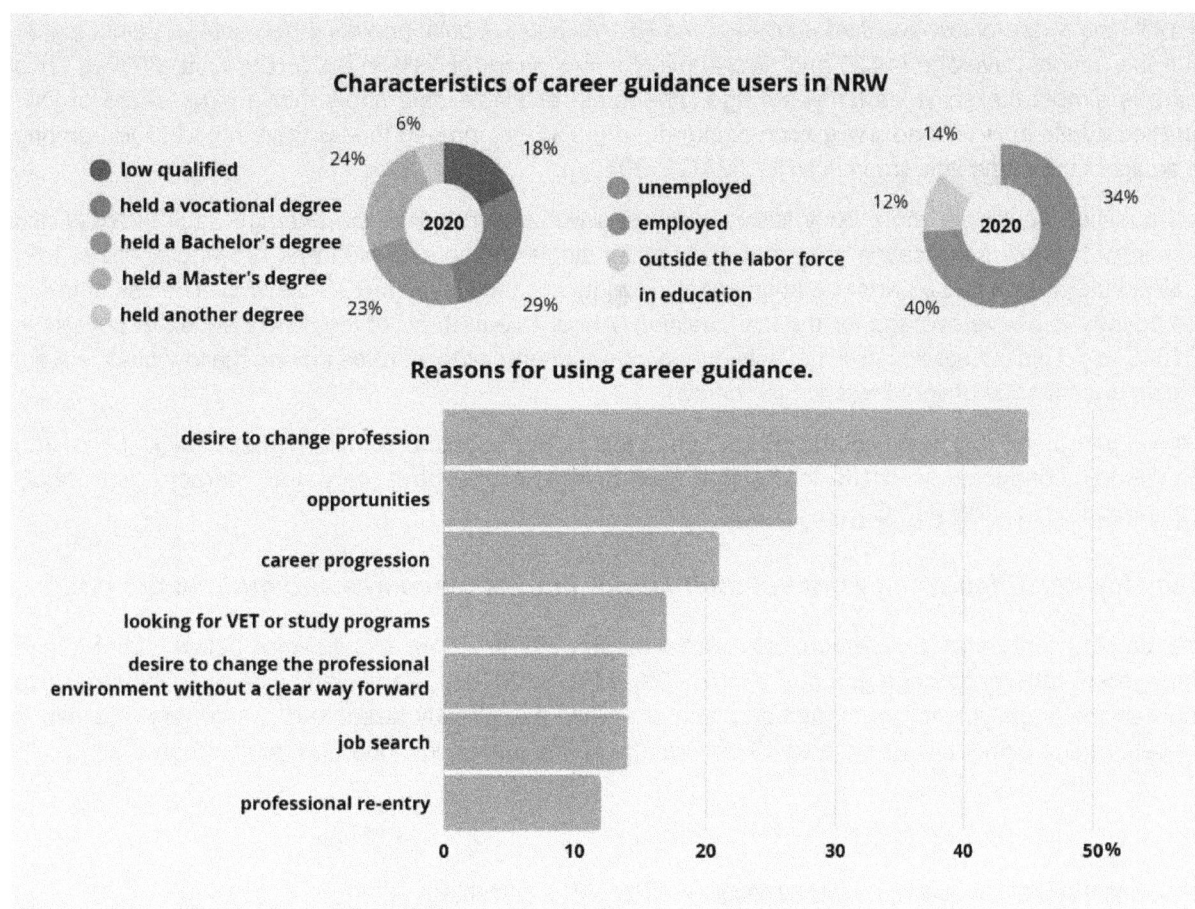

Characteristics of career guidance users in NRW

- low qualified
- held a vocational degree
- held a Bachelor's degree
- held a Master's degree
- held another degree

6%
24%
18%
2020
23%
29%

- unemployed
- employed
- outside the labor force
- in education

14%
12%
2020
40%
34%

Reasons for using career guidance.

- desire to change profession
- opportunities
- career progression
- looking for VET or study programs
- desire to change the professional environment without a clear way forward
- job search
- professional re-entry

0   10   20   30   40   50%

Note: Some figures may not add up due to rounding.
Source: G.I.B. (2021[5]), *Tabellenband 01.01.2020 bis 31.12.2020, BBE/FBA*, www.gib.nrw.de/service/downloaddatenbank/beratung-zur-beruflichen-entwicklung-fachberatung-anerkennung-bbe-fba-tabellenband-3-2020-januar-bis-dezember-2019.

A picture of the low-qualified workers in NRW

Low-qualified individuals make up almost a fifth of NRW's adult population, and 13% of employees[1] in NRW were low qualified compared to 10% in Germany on average (BA, 2020[6]). While NRW's labour market seems to absorb the large share of low-qualified adults, the future remains uncertain as the share of low-skilled jobs is likely to fall as a result of structural changes. Notably, occupations such as truck drivers and workers in warehouses and other logistics facilities or food preparation assistants are projected to decline in the near future and eventually disappear. Workers in these occupations form a substantial part of NRW's low-qualified adults. This shift underscores the need for better career guidance provision.

Low qualified workers face a multitude of disadvantages in the labour market such as low wages and poor working conditions. Poor job quality for this group provides further incentives to reskill and transition to emerging, more sustainable, occupations.

The following sections describe the composition of the NRW workforce and present an overview of the low-qualified adults' labour market conditions compared to adults with higher qualifications. As described in Annex A, the main data sources are: (i) the micro census conducted in 2018 by the federation and all federal states; and (ii) the employment statistics of the BA from between 2018 and 2021, depending on the indicator.

Most low-qualified adults have a migrant background

At 19%, the share of low-qualified adults among NRW's adult population was 4 percentage points higher than the national average (14%) and also above Berlin's share of 13% in 2020 (Eurostat, 2020[2]). This share is almost the same as ten years ago. The latest available data show that a large share of low-qualified adults in NRW had a migration background (58%),[2] compared to less than a third (30%) among all adults in the same age group in NRW (MAGS, 2020[3]).

Low-qualified adults are more likely to live in families with children than the average adult in NRW and women with a low qualification are more likely to be single mothers. A high and growing share of low-qualified individuals had a partner with an equally low qualification level (MAGS, 2020[3]). The risk of falling into poverty is above average for the low qualified. About one in three of them was at risk of poverty in 2018 (33%). This increased risk is not only due to higher unemployment rates among the low qualified, but also a consequence of very low pay (see below).

A small part of the low-qualified adults lacks the basic skills needed to acquire higher qualifications. The LEO study conducted in 2018 found that 1.36 million adults have very low literacy (*funktionale Analphabeten*) in NRW (RP Online, 2019[7]).[3]

Many low-qualified are in work but their labour market outcomes and outlook are poor

The employment rate[4] of low-qualified adults is at 57% in 2018, significantly below the average employment rate for this age group of almost 80% (MAGS, 2020[3]). Particularly striking is the large gap between the employment rate of men and women. While it is already sizeable in the general population (11 percentage point), it is as large as 19 percentage points among low-qualified adults (Figure 3.1).

Figure 3.1. The employment rate of low-qualified women is particularly low

Employment rate of low-qualified adults by gender in NRW, 2018, percentage

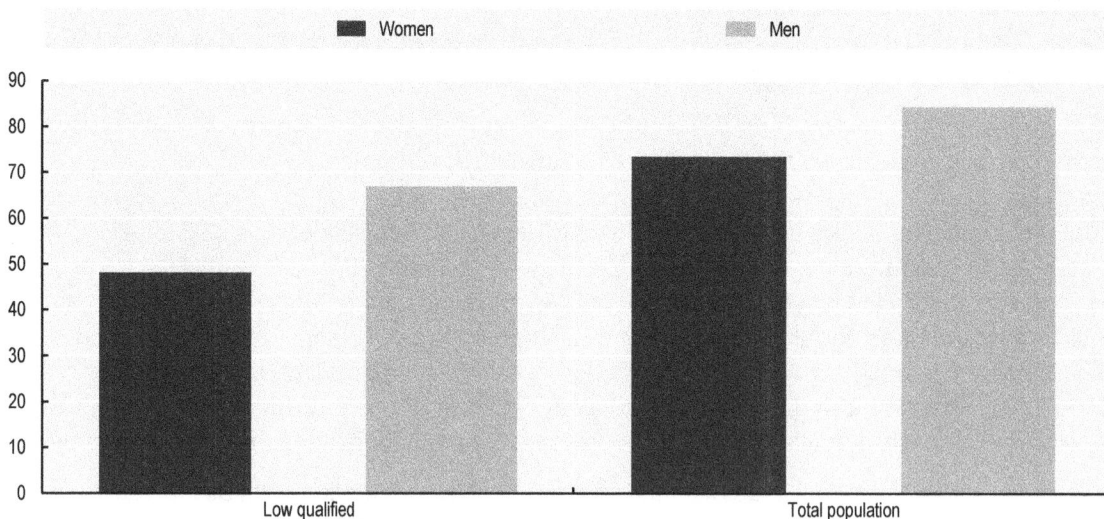

Source: IT.NRW, Mikrozensus 2018, MAGS (2020[3]), *Sozialbericht NRW 2020*, www.sozialberichte.nrw.de/sozialberichterstattung_nrw/aktuelle_berichte/SB2020.pdf.

Low-qualified adults are more likely to be unemployed than their counterparts with a formal qualification. In NRW, their unemployment rate was 24% in 2020, above the national average of 21% (BA, 2020[8]) and above the unemployment rate of adults who have completed a vocational degree (4%) and adults holding an academic degree (3%).

The vulnerability of low-qualified workers to unemployment was underscored by the COVID-19 crisis. Figure 3.2 shows that increases in unemployment varied strongly by skill level. Unemployment among adults working in helper jobs increased by 29%. Although similar increases occurred for specialists and experts, the unemployment rate of helpers is taking longer to return to pre-crisis levels.

Several other indicators confirm the difficulties that low-qualified adults face in NRW's labour market, such as the incidence of fixed-term contracts, low pay, employment in the low-wage-sector. In 2018, 57% of low-qualified workers in NRW were on fixed-term contracts, compared to 50% among those with an academic degree and 39% among those holding a vocational qualification (G.I.B., 2020[9]) and 44% of all low-qualified employed adults in NRW earned a low wage (DGB NRW, 2019[10]).

Figure 3.2. Low-skilled adults were more vulnerable to unemployment during the COVID-19 crisis

Number of unemployed adults by skill requirement level, 2019, 2020, 2021

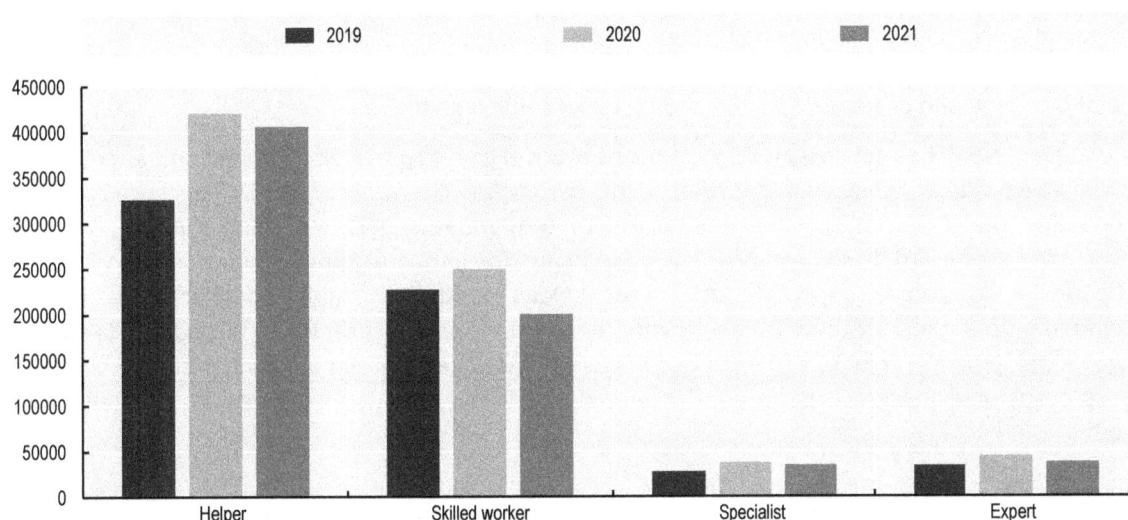

Note: The requirement level reflects the degree of complexity of the activity to be performed: Helper jobs involve assisting and semi-skilled activities (simple, less complex (routine) activities; usually no formal vocational qualification); Skilled jobs involve specialist-oriented activities (well-founded specialist knowledge and skills required; two to three years of vocational training); Specialist jobs involve complex specialist activities (special knowledge and skills, planning and management tasks, master craftsman or technician training, bachelor's degree); Expert jobs involve highly complex activities (expert knowledge, performance and management tasks, at least four years of higher education).
Source: Statistics of the Federal Employment Agency; Bundesagentur für Arbeit (2019, 2020, 2021), https://statistik.arbeitsagentur.de/SiteGlobals/Forms/Suche/Einzelheftsuche_Formular.html?nn=20894&topic_f=berufe-heft-kldb2010.

Almost 74% of the employees in NRW worked in the service sector in 2021, significantly fewer than the 87% in Berlin where the decline of manufacturing industries is more advanced. Most low-qualified adults in NRW work in transport, logistics (except driving); sales; and business organisation, such as secretarial work (BA, 2021[11]).

Labour supply strongly exceeds demand in many of the sectors that employ large shares of low-qualified adults, notably transport, logistics, protection and security (7.5 unemployed per vacancy) as well as in agriculture, forestry, animal husbandry, horticulture (ratio of 6.2), but also in commercial services, trade, distribution, tourism (5.8) (BA, 2021[12]). Transport, logistics, protection and security and commercial services, trade, distribution, tourism are among the occupations with the highest unemployment and the lowest labour demand.

Automation potential in NRW is above the German average

Recent research shows that across almost all occupations and skill-requirement levels, the automation potential (*Substituierbarkeitspotenzial*) has increased in Germany overall, including in North Rhine-Westphalia. In 2019, the share of employees working in jobs with a high potential for automation was relatively high in NRW, affecting 35.1% of all employees. This is slightly above the German average of 33.9% but for example almost twice as high as in Berlin (15% in 2016). Within NRW strong differences persist, with rates of automation risk ranging from 28% to 48%. The potential for automation is particularly high in South Westphalia, in the Bergisches Land region and in Gütersloh (IAB, 2018[13]).[5] As discussed in Chapter 2, automation risk is high for those working in manufacturing as well as low-skilled service jobs with a high-routine component – notably, helper jobs where low-qualified adults are over-represented.

Career guidance offers in NRW

In the context of the changes described above and the particular vulnerability of low-qualified adults, public support to providing career guidance has a central role to play in smoothing transitions and maintaining or increasing employability for low-qualified workers. Career guidance can accompany individuals throughout their (working) lives and prepare them in due time for upcoming changes.

Similar to Berlin, NRW has set up a publicly funded network of private providers that offers career guidance, the Guidance for Career Development (*Beratung zur beruflichen Entwicklung*, BBE). This core network is complemented by other programmes and providers with more specialised offers, including literacy initiatives, such as the NRW-wide Alphanet (*Alphanetz*) and the temporary programmes listed in Table 3.1 and support for companies, especially SMEs (see below). In addition, many small-scale projects are conducted in different regions in NRW every year, some of which focus on low-qualified adults who are already in employment (Table 3.2). In a context of severe shortage of skilled workers in the metal industry or the care sector alongside a large pool of unskilled adults, upskilling initiatives have often proven successful.

The BBE network, along with programmes by VHS, social partners, BA (LBBiE) and some smaller programmes can be found on a NRW-wide centralised career guidance platform. Apart from the search engine, the platform offers online guidance, information regarding available programmes and financial incentives as well as seminars and training courses.

Table 3.1. Temporary literacy programmes

Original name	English name	Financing bodies	Years	Region	Objective	Link
Gruwe	Gruwe	ESF, MAGS	2015-18	NRW	Strengthen work-oriented basic education for employees in SMEs	https://www.gruwe-nrw.de/
Sozialpartner gemeinsam für arbeitsorientierte Grundbildung in NRW	Social partners together for work-oriented basic education in NRW	MAGS	2020-22	NRW	Social partners support management & employee representatives in the implementation of basic education measures in companies	https://grundbildung-nrw.de
Verbundprojekt SESAM	Network project SESAM	BMBF	2012-15	NRW	Sensitise and motivate companies and their employees to implement workplace-oriented basic education programmes and support them in the implementation	www.sesam-nrw.de
Grundbildung mit Erwerbswelt-erfahrung	Basic education with work experience	ESF, MAGS, MKW	2007-16	NRW	Improve basic education of disadvantaged (young) adults	www.mags.nrw/sites/default/files/asset/document/esf_evaluation_grundbildung_mit_erwerbswelterfahrung.pdf

Table 3.2. Selected small scale projects for low-qualified employees

Original name	English name	Financing bodies	Years	Region	Objective	Link
Nächste Station Facharbeiter	Next station skilled worker	ESF	2017-19	Region East-Westphalia-Lippe	Accompany long standing low-qualified employees on their way to pass the official skilled labour examination in the metal industry	https://www.fachkraefteinitiative-nrw.de/einzelregionen/ostwestfalen-lippe/projekte-nachste-station-facharbeiter-al-2019-09-17.pdf
Zukunft Pflege NiederRhein – Fachkräfte-sicherung in der Altenpflege	Future Care LowerRhine – Securing skilled workers in geriatric care	ESF	2012/13	Region Lower Rhine	Coaching during 10 qualification modules for employees, their representatives and management	https://www.fachkraefteinitiative-nrw.de/einzelregionen/niederrhein/niederrhein-innowise-2012-06-04.pdf
Interkulturelles Coaching für Menschen mit Migrations-hintergrund	Intercultural coaching for individuals with a migration background	ESF	2012	Region Westphalian Ruhr Area	Individual coaching for adults during the preparation for the official examination to become a certified educator; networking and placement support after completion	https://www.fachkraefteinitiative-nrw.de/einzelregionen/westfaelisches-ruhrgebiet/grieseler.pdf

The services of the Guidance for career development are being reviewed with an emphasis on improving quality

In NRW, the career guidance network has been set up via the ESF-funded programme Guidance for Career Development (*Beratung zur beruflichen Entwicklung*, BBE). The career guidance services they provide are open to all adults, including, but not specifically targeted at, low-qualified adults. The political discussion has revolved around the need to reskill and upskill adult workers who are particularly at risk due to structural changes, but so far, no programmes are planned for this specific target group.

NRW is sub-divided into 16 labour market regions (*Arbeitsmarktregionen*), each of which has a regional agency that is responsible for co-ordinating the BBE career guidance offices in their labour market region. Currently, 125 offices are distributed across the regions to ensure easy face-to-face access to career guidance everywhere in NRW. The regional agencies can be located at offices of different actors in a region, such as the commune, the county (*Landkreis*) or a CET provider's facilities. Equally financed via ESF funds, they implement the labour policies in the regions and inform the ministry about developments on site.

The co-ordination of these regional agencies is under the responsibility of the Gesellschaft für innovative Beschäftigungsförderung mbH, G.I.B., a subsidiary owned by the state government. G.I.B. generally supports the Ministry of Labour, Health and Social Affairs of the State of North Rhine-Westphalia, (*Ministerium für Arbeit, Gesundheit und Soziales*, MAGS), in implementing the labour policy, one part of which is CET and career guidance. G.I.B. regularly meets with the 16 regional agencies to co-ordinate the provision of career guidance in NRW and offer exchanges on common issues.

The G.I.B. set quality standards according to which it runs monitoring schemes for internal information. These quality standards are useful within NRW, but they are not co-ordinated to the quality of providers in neighbouring federal states, such as Rhineland-Palatinate or Lower Saxony or the rest of Germany. In the effort to maintain high quality provision, the G.I.B. also offers training for career guidance counsellors. Each counsellor must complete a three-day basic training course when taking up duties and other courses are offered on demand, such as courses on digital tools and the provision of remote career guidance services or on the recognition of qualifications acquired abroad.

The MAGS fully funds the career guidance services provided by the BBE offices. Currently an office receives a fixed amount of EUR 55 for every hour of career guidance it provides. The offices can use their existing staff, hire new staff or freelancers. The service must be provided free of charge to the user.

Career guidance services include counselling on topics such as:

- Professional reorientation.
- Professional improvement.
- CET.
- Obtain general and vocational formal degrees in the form of second chance education (*Nachholen eines (Berufs-)Abschlusses*).
- Return to work (after a family career break).
- Competence assessment using various procedures (to determine formally and informally acquired competences).
- The recognition of foreign qualifications (possibly referral to the specialised counselling centre, see below).

BBE also provides guidance on NRW's education and training leave as well as on the various financial incentives available in NRW.

With the start of the ESF funding period 2021-27, the G.I.B. launched a new call for tenders to select service providers. With the objective of improving the quality of the services, the new offices will have to comply with revised quality criteria and the hourly allowance will increase from EUR 55 to EUR 68. Increased emphasis will also be given to the provision of integrated services as a selection criterion of the new tender procedure. The call for tender specifies that, preferably, the new BBE offices should be well connected with providers of other guidance services, such as debt counselling, psychosocial counselling, housing counselling, neighbourhood counselling etc., so that career guidance users can easily be redirected to the appropriate service.

Some of the BBE counselling centres have specialised on the recognition of foreign qualifications (*Fachberatung zur Anerkennung ausländischer Berufsqualifikationen*, FBA). Counsellors help with doubts about whether a qualification can be recognised, whether a recognition would improve the employment possibilities and they also help directly with the application for recognition and with financing it as well as with finding CET options in the case of partial recognition.

The BBE does not currently run any outreach activities. Several outreach pilots have been tested in the past few years but all were discontinued, partly due to high administrative costs. On the other hand, significant outreach efforts accompany the career guidance activities run by the Counselling Centres Work (*Beratungsstellen Arbeit*), launched at the beginning of 2021 (MAGS, 2021[14]). The focus is placed on adults looking for work, but support is also offered to workers in precarious employment e.g. in the meat and agriculture industry or in logistics centres, who are often (formally) low qualified.

Centralised access to career guidance services available in the state is facilitated by an online platform

Online career guidance programmes can be found through the career guidance platform Continuing Education and Training Guidance in North Rhine-Westphalia (*Weiterbildungsberatung* in *Nordrhein-Westfalen*). Similar to the Berlin model, the portal lists and provides access to most career guidance opportunities. It advertises offers by the BBE's sub-contracted private providers including those specialised on counselling on the recognition of qualifications acquired abroad and the offices providing counselling on specific financial incentives, such as the NRW education cheque (*Bildungsscheck*) or the federal education grant (Bildungsprämie).

Apart from the core BBE network, the website also includes programmes by a range of other providers. LBBiE can now be found on the website (see Box 3.1), as well as education and counselling centres by social partners and the VHS. The German Trade Union Federation (*Deutscher Gewerkschaftsbund*, DGB) and the chamber of skilled crafts (*Handwerkskammer*), for example, run education centres in Düsseldorf. Some business associations are also part of the network such as the business association Essen (EUV). Equally, the Work and Life programme by DGB and VHS is based at a local office that can be found via the website. Smaller programmes, such as the further training support for inland navigation operators (*Fortbildungsförderung für Binnenschiffer*), appear too. In total, more than 250 counselling offices offer their services on the platform.

The most obvious difference compared to the online platform run by the career guidance network in Berlin is that the individuals looking for career guidance need to have a certain prior knowledge of their needs, as well as on the topic they need career guidance on. The users can choose to browse the career guidance offers based on either the topic they are interested in, such as returning to work (*Berufsrückkehr*), guidance concerning foreign educational qualifications or based on the administrative instrument they expect to use, such as the education cheque (*Bildungsscheck NRW*), the nationwide education grant (*Bildungsprämie*) or vocational upskilling (*Aufstiegs-BAföG*).

Box 3.1. Integration of LBBiE in NRW

As in most federal states, the provision of LBBiE in NRW has started in 2021, in parallel to the existing career guidance programmes provided by the BBE and the integration is ongoing. Both BBE and LBBiE focus on guidance for individuals' professional development and the guidance sessions are not geared towards a specific objective (as e.g. a rapid integration into the labour market). The design of the BA's LBBiE was initially inspired by the BBE in NRW, which is why the two programmes are very similar. The NRW BBE is ESF funded and since ESF funding can only be used for programmes that do not exist yet in a given country or region, its long-term future is uncertain. In the short term, BBE has been prolonged for another two years until 2023.

Advice for companies to encourage the skill development of employees is provided through targeted programmes and networks

As in Berlin, SMEs have access to support on adult learning (*Qualifizierungsberatung*). In NRW, it is part of the ESF-financed Potential Counselling (*Potentialberatung*) unless the company chooses to use the federal programme "*unternehmensWert: Mensch*" described in Chapter 1. Potential Counselling includes a broad range of topics including adult learning but also work organisation, digitalisation and health and safety. The programme is offered by around 100 private and social partner-run counselling centres that can be found via a dedicated search engine.[6] Companies can request financial support for up to ten counselling days where half of the counsellor's daily rate is to be paid by the company and the other half is covered by the programme.[7] As in Berlin, the counsellors help to assess the competences of employees and to build sustainable in-company CET and knowledge management. The objective is to complement the company's innovation goals with developing a consistent training strategy.

In the context of the federal programme for the development of CET networks (*Bundesprogramm zum Aufbau von Weiterbildungsverbünden*) described in Chapter 1, six networks have been set up in NRW to provide support to employers in selected sectors or regions. The following table gives an overview of the networks:

Table 3.3. CET networks under the federal programme in NRW

Original name	English name	Actors involved	Focus
geWiN (gemeinsam Weiterbilden im Netzwerk)	geWiN (training jointly in the network)	proPerson Transfergesellschaft; KIST e.V.	-
KoWeMi – Koordinierungsstelle zur Weiterbildung in der Mikrotechnik	KoWeMi – Co-ordination Office for CET in Micro-technology	PROSPEKTIV – Gesellschaft für betriebliche Zukunftsgestaltungen mbH; IVAM Fachverband für Mikrotechnik	Micro- and nano-technology
PEaP 4.0 – Weiterbildungsverbund Personalentwicklung 4.0 ambulante Pflege	PEaP 4.0 – CET Network HR Development 4.0 outpatient care	Bildungsinstitut im Gesundheitswesen gGmbH; maxQ in bfw Unternehmen für Bildung; Tutoolio GmbH; MedEcon Ruhr	Outpatient care
proWeiterbildung PLUS – systematisch, regional, vernetzt	proCET PLUS – systematic, regional, networked	Wirtschaftsförderung für den Kreis Unna mbH; Netzwerk Industrie RuhrOst e.V.	-
Weiterbildungsplattform für Industrie 4.0 –Technologien	CETplatform for the industry 4.0 – Technologies	Universität Duisburg-Essen; Digital Campus Zollverein e.V.; EWG mbH; neusta software development west; TÜV Nord Bildungs GmbH NRW; GSI – Gesellschaft für Schweißtechnik mbH	Technologies
Weiterbildungsverbund für Digitalisierung und KI in Ostwestfalen-Lippe (OWL)	CET Network for Digitalisation and AI in OWL	Initiative für Beschäftigung OWL e.V.; ELHA Maschinenbau Liemke KG; gpdm GmbH	Digitalisation and AI
Weiterbildungsverbund.Ruhr	CETnetwork.Ruhr	VHS Witten Wetter Herdecke; VHS Bochum; Gesellschaft für Beschäftigung Herne; Bildungsinstitut Vogel	-

Note: Since all networks are approved but most are still being implemented, information on specific foci may not always be available.

Structural programmes to guide transitions

Some regions within NRW are particularly affected by structural changes. One of them is the **Rhenish Mining Area (*Rheinisches Revier*)**, where the lignite-fired power plants (*Braunkohlekraftwerke*) are located. An economic and structural programme has been set up to manage the structural change in this district, as well as in three more in other parts of Germany (IRR - Innovationsregion Rheinisches Revier GmbH, 2021[15]).

In the Rhenish Mining Area, priorities are divided in seven district knots (*Revierknoten*), committees composed of experts on the respective topic, which have been set up jointly by the Federal Ministry for Economic Affairs and Energy and the State Ministry of Economy, Innovation, Digitalisation and Energy (MWIDE) in 2019 and the roll-out is still ongoing. The so-called Future Agency for the Rhenish Mining Area is responsible for the implementation of the strategic goals in each knot with a budget of almost EUR 15 billion.

The programme aims at facilitating access to the existing CET structures and to network these structures better. It supports the setup of a "Learning Factory" that provides career guidance for individuals and support for employers as well as learning possibilities and equipment, all at the same facility.

A region that has undergone similar challenges is the **Ruhr area (*Ruhrgebiet*)** where structural changes have been ongoing for several decades already. In the 1950s, the Ruhr region had a bustling economy driven by coal mining and heavy industries. Over the following decades, however, employment in the production sector dropped sharply, pushing the entire region into a crisis. Several development programmes were adopted but only when unemployment was already high and when people's contexts had changed while their skills had not. The approach used in the Rhenish District is expected to include lessons from this period and follow a preventive concept, rather than a reactive one, including career guidance to motivate adults working in mining to retrain.

Integrating career guidance, validation and partial qualifications

The OECD report on Continuing Education and Training in Germany emphasised the need to better integrate the areas of career guidance, validation and partial qualifications in Germany. At the regional level, NRW has some initiatives in place that use this approach of integrated offers.

One example is the Cologne Education Model (*Kölner Bildungsmodell*).[8] The Municipal Alliance for Jobs in Cologne started this initiative with the aim to help meet demand for skilled workers in the Cologne region as well as to enable young adults to acquire a vocational qualification and to integrate them into the labour market in a sustainable way. To achieve these two goals, the Cologne Education Model offers modular qualification to adults of 25 years old and above. Before starting a qualification module, an individual takes part in a profiling phase, where a potential analysis (*Potenzialanalyse*) containing several kinds of tests and a matching between the individuals interests and an occupation is used as an initial assessment of suitability. This profiling phase is followed by 4-week long period during which the individual can try out different work environments. Once the individual has completed all the modules, the Model also supports with the preparation for the final exam to acquire the formal qualification.

Over the entire period, coaches support the participating individuals. These coaches are considered a vital factor in the success of the Model. They support the participants in all steps of the qualification from planning their learning activities to the preparation for the final exam. They intervene e.g. in case of adjustment difficulties during internships and help with personal problems. Coaching participants over time through spells of employment or unemployment, as long as participation in the Cologne Education Model continues.

A recent pilot took place at NRW level that also included career guidance, partial qualification and the preparation for the final exams to obtain a formal qualification, accompanied by coaches throughout. Financed by the federal state of NRW, ESF and the Job Centres, it did, however, target only unemployed adults and job seekers who cannot or do not want to commit to a two- or three-years-long formal qualification.

Use of career guidance in NRW

In NRW, the G.I.B. collects and publishes data on the use of career guidance. The data cover the provision of the BBE programme and the Advice on the Recognition of Foreign Professional Qualifications programme, FBA. Data are collected on the number of career guidance sessions that have been held and the number of individuals using guidance for the first time in a given year. Data are also available on their socio-economic background, the advertisement channel through which they found the career guidance offer and their reasons for using guidance as well as the outcomes and consequences of the guidance processes. The latest data refer to 2020, data for the first half of 2021 confirm the trends.

Counsellors held a total of 13 279 career guidance sessions in 2020 (Statistik der G.I.B. mbH, 2021[5]). This compares to almost 19 000 sessions held in 2019 prior to the COVID-19 pandemic. Of the sessions held in 2020, 8 728 took place within the framework of the BBE programme (66%), 3 220 within the FBA programme (24%), 585 as a combination of the two programmes and 746 without allocation to a specific programme. By far most BBE counselling sessions took place in the region of Cologne, while most FBA sessions took place in the Westphalian Ruhr Area (*Westfälisches Ruhrgebiet*).

Women, migrants and refugees are the most frequent users of career guidance services

More detailed data on the users of BBE and FBA are available for the group of new entrants into counselling in 2020. In total these were 5 256, 62% of which used BBE. Unlike in Berlin, the majority of users in both programmes were female. Overall, most users were between 25 and 49 years old, with more adults aged 50+ using BBE than those 24 or younger. Forty-seven percent of BBE users had a migrant background. Seventy-four percent of FBA users held a nationality form a non-EU country and 46% had a refugee background. Eighteen percent of all users were low qualified, in line with the proportion of low-qualified adults in NRW (19%). Given their disproportional need for support, there is however room for expanding the share of this group. The users' employment status differed strongly depending on the career guidance programme. Almost 50% of the adults using BBE guidance were in employment, 27% unemployed and 12% outside the labour market. In the FBA programme, only 15% were in employment while more than 50% were unemployed.

The most common field of work that the employed users worked in or that the unemployed used to work in is commercial services, trade of goods, distribution and hotel and tourism (29%). Almost as many (26%) came from health, social affairs, teaching and education occupations. For comparison, only 7% of the users worked in raw material extraction, production and manufacturing despite the significant changes that these sectors are undergoing.

The majority of BBE users are in employment, thus the main motivation for seeking career guidance is the desire to change profession (45%) rather than looking for an opportunity to re-enter the labour market (12%) (Figure 3.3). Another 14% reported the wish of changing something in their professional environment without having a concrete way forward, others wished to improve their professional situation. A significant share also accessed career guidance for support in identifying CET opportunities (27%) and vocational training or studies (17%). Most career guidance sessions lead to job and internship searches, or training participation, although it is not known whether training ultimately leads to an occupational/sectoral change. FBA guidance, which has the recognition of foreign professional qualifications as objective, led in 52% of the cases to an application for recognition or assessment of professional qualifications acquired abroad to the competent body. Users started qualification measures in 14% of the cases.

Just as in Berlin, adults learned about the BBE programme mostly via colleagues, friends, acquaintances and family (35%). The second most used channel was the internet followed by the two BA centres: Jobcentres and employment agencies (13%). Also, 12% of users were directed to career guidance by CET providers.

Figure 3.3. Most adults use career guidance for their professional development

New admissions to the BBE by central reason for using career guidance, 2020, percentage

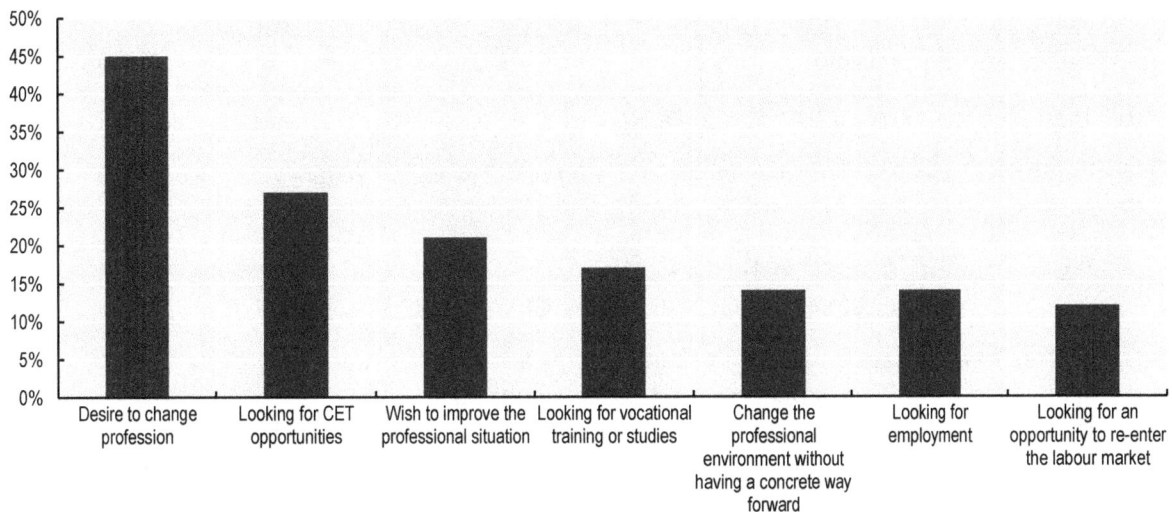

Note: Several answers possible; question is only asked for the BBE programme.
Source: G.I.B. (2021[5]), *Tabellenband 01.01.2020 bis 31.12.2020, BBE/FBA.*

References

BA (2021), *Arbeitsmarktreport NRW 2021*, https://statistik.arbeitsagentur.de/SiteGlobals/Forms/Suche/Einzelheftsuche_Formular.html?topic_f=amr-amr&r_f=bl_Nordrhein-Westfalen. [12]

BA (2021), *Beschäftigte nach Berufen*, https://statistik.arbeitsagentur.de/SiteGlobals/Forms/Suche/Einzelheftsuche_Formular.html;jsessionid=63414B7309EAA6B9744BC0BDFB197A99?nn=20894&topic_f=beschaeftigung-sozbe-bo-heft. [11]

BA (2020), *Qualifikationsspezifische Arbeitslosenquoten*, https://statistik.arbeitsagentur.de/SiteGlobals/Forms/Suche/Einzelheftsuche_Formular.html?nn=1610088&topic_f=alo-qualiquote. [8]

BA (2020), *Qualifikationsspezifische Arbeitslosenquoten (Jahreszahlen)*, https://statistik.arbeitsagentur.de/SiteGlobals/Forms/Suche/Einzelheftsuche_Formular.html?nn=1610088&topic_f=alo-qualiquote. [6]

DGB NRW (2019), *Der Niedriglohnsektor in NRW*, https://nrw.dgb.de/++co++1d1abcfc-2359-11eb-81c3-001a4a16011a. [10]

DIE (2019), *Inhaltliche und strukturelle Anforderungen an eine Weiterbildungslandschaft im Rahmen der digitalen Transformation der Arbeitswelt*, http://www.landtag.nrw.de/portal/WWW/dokumentenarchiv/Dokument/MMI17-186.pdf. [1]

Eurostat (2020), *Population by educational attainment level, sex and NUTS 2 regions*, https://ec.europa.eu/eurostat/databrowser/view/edat_lfse_04/default/table?lang=en. [2]

G.I.B. (2020), *Arbeitsmarktreport NRW 2020, Bericht 4/2020*, http://www.gib.nrw.de/themen/monitoring-und-evaluation/g-i-b-bericht-4-2020-arbeitsmarktreport-nrw-2020. [9]

IAB (2018), *IAB-Regional Nordrhein-Westfalen 1/2018*. [13]

IAB NRW (2019), *Substituierbarkeitspotenziale in Nordrhein-Westfalen 2019 – Ausgewählte Ergebnisse*. [4]

IRR - Innovationsregion Rheinisches Revier GmbH (2021), *Durch Wissen Innovationen schaffen*, https://www.rheinisches-revier.de/themen/revierknoten-innovation-und-bildung. [15]

MAGS (2021), *Beratungsstellen Arbeit unterstützen arbeitslose und prekär beschäftigte Menschen - Baustein für Netzwerk gegen Arbeitsausbeutung*, http://www.mags.nrw/beratungsstellen-arbeit-auftakt (accessed on 8 December 2021). [14]

MAGS (2020), *Sozialbericht NRW 2020*, http://www.sozialberichte.nrw.de/sozialberichterstattung_nrw/aktuelle_berichte/SB2020.pdf. [3]

OECD (2021), *Continuing Education and Training in Germany*, Getting Skills Right, OECD Publishing, Paris, https://doi.org/10.1787/1f552468-en. [16]

RP Online (2019), *Jeder achte Erwachsene in NRW kann nicht richtig lesen und schreiben*, https://rp-online.de/nrw/panorama/nrw-analphabet-ist-jeder-achte-erwachsene-verband-kritisiert-landesregierung_aid-45665737. [7]

Statistik der G.I.B. mbH (2021), *Tabellenband 01.01.2020 bis 31.12.2020, BBE/FBA*. [5]

Notes

[1] Employees subject to compulsory social insurance (Sozialversicherungspflichtig Beschäftigte).

[2] In 2017, a new micro census law (MZG 2017) was introduced, implementing the collection of data on an individual's extended migration background: Individuals with a migration background include all persons living in Germany without German citizenship and also persons who either do not themselves have German citizenship by birth or have at least one parent to whom this applies and who immigrated or were born after 1949 (cf. Statistisches Bundesamt 2019: 4). Foreigners are therefore a subgroup of individuals with a migration background.

[3] For more information on literacy in Germany see OECD (2021[16]).

[4] *Erwerbstätigenquote*, according to the definition of the Micro census.

[5] Update sent by IAB via e-mail for 2019.

[6] www.gib.nrw.de/themen/arbeitsgestaltung-und-sicherung/potentialberatung/beraterdatenbank.

[7] up to a maximum of EUR 500 per counselling day.

[8] www.koelner-bildungsmodell.de.

4 Towards a better career guidance system

This chapter discusses the challenges that have been identified throughout the report. They focus particularly on ensuring equal and easy access to career guidance for low-qualified workers and their employers; on providing high quality career guidance nationwide; and on strengthening networking among the different stakeholders. This discussion leads to recommendations that propose ways forward and aspects to consider when introducing reforms to the current career guidance system at national level and in the different federal states.

Introduction

In line with the vision of a "CET Republic (*Weiterbildungsrepublik*)" proclaimed by the previous German Government in the context of the NWS in 2021 and pursued by the new government, all actors involved in CET need to work together towards creating a culture of lifelong learning across the country. Many high quality offers for various target groups already exist, but take-up is low, especially among the low qualified. A lack of knowledge about CET options, the lack of awareness of its benefits and anxiety towards a return to the classroom are among the biggest barriers to training among adults.

Career guidance stands to play a crucial role in achieving this objective, as it can help address many of the dispositional and situational barriers that prevents adults from engaging in training as well as provide support in navigating the available training offers.

The report identifies low-qualified workers as a group that is ill served by existing programmes. While individuals in this group are in work, their labour market outcomes are often poor and the outlook ahead is bleak due to technological advances and other structural changes that threaten the sectors in which they are most often employed.

This section provides recommendations of how to make career guidance more relevant to them, by preventing skills obsolesce, fostering retraining, facilitating transitions to emerging sectors and occupations and recognising uncertified skills. Wherever possible, a developmental approach bears the most promising results by aiming at the persons' involvement in processes that will support them. The recommendations focus on access to career guidance, quality of guidance and networking among the different stakeholders.

Streamline and connect existing career guidance offers

Streamline current provision under a 'single brand' at national level: Career guidance services vary significantly across federal states and sometimes across regions in the same state. There are currently no co-ordination mechanisms to enhance consistency, creating imbalances in access to and quality of provision. To address this challenge, the regional and local networks should be complemented by an overarching framework at the national level and the creation of a single career guidance brand. Such an initiative would streamline current provision and close any regional supply gaps. Operating under a single brand would increase the visibility of existing programmes, improve transparency for individuals looking for career guidance and ensure that individuals receive the most appropriate guidance for their specific needs. The success of this framework would strongly rely on the definition of common quality standards. These standards would allow creating a high quality brand with reliably good offers nationwide. The national brand could involve social partners and other local stakeholders, given their key role in the provision of career guidance.

At the national level, policy makers, associations of career guidance providers as well as the main employers' and employees' associations should come together to define a global vision for the brand and the related quality standards. Assessing and collating the needs of individuals and employers, matching them with the goals of policy makers would allow for a common understanding of what constitutes high-quality career guidance and would foster services in line with the projected needs of the labour markets (see recommendation on enabling providers).

The need for a national strategy on vocational and continuing education that respects local diversity has recently found support by the Education Alliance of SMEs (*Bundesverband mittelständische Wirtschaft, Unternehmerverband Deutschlands e.V.*) (BVMW, 2021[1]). The shortage of skilled workers, the large share of early school leavers – particularly following the COVID-19 crisis – and difficulties finding apprentices have put SMEs in a difficult position when it comes to hiring skilled labour, leading to a call for a more consistent career guidance offer nationwide.

Ensure the sustainability of regional and sectoral networking initiatives: Networking initiatives play a crucial role in bringing together and co-ordinating provision at regional level. As networks, such as the ones initiated by the BMAS, evolve, guaranteeing continuity is a crucial challenge: the concern that successful pilots may be discontinued risks discouraging actors from investing further in the networks. Trust in the co-ordination and fair co-operation among all actors take time to develop but are key for the success of these initiatives. It is therefore important that the government starts considering how the networks can be sustained beyond the four-years funding period, signalling long-term engagement to all actors.

Support existing career guidance offers at federal state level to engage with low-qualified workers: Despite having access to most career guidance programmes, low-qualified workers use it less than their higher qualified peers do. Where low-qualified workers cannot be reached through their employers, the individual career guidance offers at federal state level should include a service that specialises on reaching out to this specific target group. Low-qualified workers often face a combination of barriers to CET that are particularly difficult to overcome and require skilled counsellors with a long-term commitment and well-connected services to deal holistically with multiple barriers. It is particularly important that referrals between actors and sometimes even between different services of the same actor work smoothly. Publicly provided career guidance is particularly important when neither the employer nor the individual have an intrinsic motivation to initiate training.

Box 4.1. Focus on low-qualified adults

Iceland

In Iceland, Lifelong Learning Centres provide education and career counselling with a specific focus on low skilled adults. A key strength of the centres are the skills of their staff: career guidance advisors typically have a diploma or a master's degree in education or vocational counselling. The objective is to strengthen the variety and quality of education and encourage general participation in lifelong learning and education. The reach of the centres is broad: there are dozens of Lifelong Learning Centres around the country including in sparsely populated areas, which conduct around 10 000 career guidance sessions with adults with low qualification levels per year. All adults over 20 are eligible, but preferential support is given to low-qualified workers in the tourism sector; low-qualified workers in SMEs; low-income workers; the unemployed with a particular focus on the long-term unemployed.

Source: OECD (2021[2]), *Career Guidance for Adults in a Changing World of Work*, https://doi.org/10.1787/9a94bfad-en.

Strengthen outreach measures

According to the SCGA, only 36% of German low-qualified adults used career guidance on their own initiative. In order to engage this target group more in the use of career guidance, outreach measures have been piloted in some federal states, but always remain limited in scope. The right to CET guidance established in the Skills Development Opportunities Act (QCG) also requires outreach to potential beneficiaries. The outreach measures for low-qualified workers should be integrated in the general outreach and guidance activities and focus specifically on regions and sectors threatened by automation. The following approaches could be used to reach out to low-qualified workers:

- Reaching out to workers who are already taking part in CET or language courses and offer them career guidance directly, as it is done in some Adult Education Centres.

- Outreach through existing services for vulnerable adults and using social workers, teachers, hospital staff, library staff, etc., as mediators may prove preferable to implementing new ad-hoc outreach campaigns.
- Where they exist, community apps used by associations of neighbours could be used to advertise career guidance programmes.
- Broad public awareness campaigns seem to be more effective in attracting refugees, but less so for native adults.
- Outreach through social media has also proven effective in several countries, particular for younger workers (Box 4.2).

Box 4.2. Outreach via social media

Examples from different countries show how social media can be used in outreach strategies:

In **Belgium**, the PES (*Forem*) uses Facebook to communicate with young people and promote its services. Additionally, YouTube is used to share videos about PES services and Twitter is used to highlight new training opportunities.

In **Italy**, the Youth Guarantee Communications Plan 2014-15 used specific web- and mobile campaigns to share information to specific target groups.

In **Portugal**, some Qualifica Centers are using social networks, such as Facebook to advertise their services. Via videos and regular updates, they keep their followers engaged and present the centres as an open space that is accessible for everyone. This aims to engage adults who may have anxiety towards re-entering formal learning environments.

Source: CEDEFOP (2021[3]), *How can you integrate LMI in your guidance activities?*, www.cedefop.europa.eu/en/tools/resources-guidance/toolkit/how-can-you-integrate-lmi-in-your-guidance-activities; Centro Qualifica Azambuja (2021[4]), www.facebook.com/centroqualifica.azambuja.3.

Improve the framework conditions of career guidance services for low-qualified workers

In order to increase the use and effectiveness of career guidance, it is crucial that services are designed to fit with the needs of the target group. Low-qualified adults are a heterogeneous group, including a large share of women, migrants, refugees and workers in helper jobs. This requires tailored career guidance services that can be adjusted to the individual's needs. While highly individualised measures can be disproportionately costly, the following measures address very specific barriers:

Introduce career guidance leave to support users who work: The expansion of the paid CET leave recommended in (OECD, 2021[5]) should be complemented by the possibility to use the leave to participate in career guidance sessions. Particularly low-qualified workers are unlikely to consult guidance programmes on their own initiative in their free time. Their take-up of CET leave is low and a stronger promotion of free guidance during working hours could significantly increase take-up. Financial incentives should be paid to the employer to compensate for the reduction in production during the time of the career guidance session.

Box 4.3. Career guidance leave in other countries

Denmark

Learners may use training leave funded through the State Grant System for Adult Training (VEU-godtgørelse) to consult guidance services relating to their education and training. When completing an Individual Competence Assessment (IKV), low skilled and middle-skilled participants aged 18-65 are entitled to a fixed allowance funded by the state which also funds training leave. Only the funding arrangements are regulated by law; the social partners may regulate all other issues concerning training leave through collective agreements.

Netherlands

In the Netherlands, training is seen primarily as a responsibility of the social partners. Many large companies have social agreements (CAO) with career guidance facilities that allow workers to have time off work to consult guidance advisors. However, significant differences in the regulation of training leave exist between sectors.

Source: OECD (2021[2]), *Career Guidance for Adults in a Changing World of Work*, https://doi.org/10.1787/9a94bfad-en.

Systematically implement the concept of one-stop-shops: Given the multiple barriers faced by the target group, career guidance programmes should systematically follow a one-stop-shop approach that helps adults identify their development needs and matching CET opportunities while also addressing any other barriers they might face (financing, health issues, care responsibilities, time-related issues etc.). These services should continue to support individuals while in training, through counselling, coaching and other support to limit dropouts.

For young adults up to 25 years the so-called Youth Employment Agencies (*Jugendberufsagenturen*), cross-jurisdictional alliances of different social service providers, serve as one-stop-shops for services needed to successfully master transitions from school to employment (BA, 2021[6]). Similar approaches could be developed for adults so that guidance on CET is provided along with employment services, migration services, judicial assistance etc. Where a reorganisation of the career guidance structure is not realistic (yet), the frontend visible to the user should still appear as a one-stop-shop while behind the scenes the different stakeholders improve referrals among them. For instance, given the BA's limited resources, the job centres may not be in a position to offer physical one-stop-shop services to adults but could rely on collaboration with and referrals to other actors, such as the federal states' career guidance providers where available.

Grant flexibility in the use and combination of different delivery channels: While digital and online career guidance should continue to be used, it is indispensable to ensure the availability of face-to-face guidance opportunities. Since online solutions often require fewer resources, there may be the risk of a shift towards these offers, which may be difficult to access for many low-qualified and especially low-income adults. Increasing evidence shows that personal career guidance provision, through coaching and mentoring schemes, is one of the most effective strategies to engage low-qualified workers. Germany should thus expand and systematise work-based career guidance and mentoring schemes (OECD, 2021[5]). In addition to initiatives by the social partners such as the CET mentors (*Weiterbildungsmentoren*) and coaching organised via the Participation Opportunities Act (*Teilhabechancengesetz*), funding should be made available nationwide to enable providers to develop effective initiatives in co-operation with local partners who have access to the target group.

Integrate career guidance with the validation of skills and partial qualifications: As described in (OECD, 2021[5]), policy developments on career guidance, validation of skills and CET not always occur in a joined-up manner. This can hinder a smooth transition from one step to the next for the individual and disrupt upskilling and reskilling processes. Establishing a working group, as proposed in the report, composed by key stakeholders of the three policy areas could explore linkages and issue recommendations to the German Government on further actions to be taken.

Pursue the further development of the BA towards a public employment and CET service (*Agentur für Arbeit und Weiterbildung*)

Following the idea of a CET republic, the BA has a great potential to become a public employment *and CET* service. The current expansion of the BA's LBBiE shows the commitment by policy makers to support this strategy and open access to CET guidance even more. Guidance on employment and CET for workers can help prevent unemployment before it arises. The following recommendations apply to broadening the role of the BA:

Increase the capacities of Job Centres to provide career guidance: Currently, the approach to guidance is still very different in Employment Agencies (*Arbeitsagenturen*) compared to Job Centres[1] in most locations. The capacity of case workers to provide individualised advice is very limited in Job Centres, often due to the high caseload. At the same time their clients' needs are often high and their situations very complex. Where individualised career guidance cannot be provided by the caseworkers, additional support through specialised counsellors and coaches is very important. It is essential that the new or retrained counsellors under the LBBiE scheme be given the capacity – especially in terms of time – to provide the same in-depth skills analysis and develop an individualised career pathway for the individuals they are in charge of in Job Centres, leveraging the counselling tools already used in Employment Agencies. Since there will not be enough LBBiE counsellors available nationwide to cover all locations, specialised coaches can complement the counsellors' work and encourage the individuals to stay engaged.

Collect and analyse data on career guidance sessions and users: Data collection should be intensified by all guidance providers and especially by the BA. While most co-ordinated career guidance offers in the federal states (see above) collect and publish data on users and guidance sessions, no data is collected by the biggest nationwide provider of career guidance, the BA. This undermines improvements in targeting, quality as well as transparency and accountability. Matching these data with the ones collected by the federal states' offers can enable the BA to play an important role in filling regional supply gaps. In addition to the collection of data on the career guidance sessions themselves, an effort should be made to follow user outcomes. Much can be learnt to improve the provision of career guidance and ensure evidence-based policy making.

Provide support to SMEs on providing career guidance and training for low-qualified employees

Well-designed support policies can assist companies in assessing the skills of their employees, planning training provision and ultimately increase productivity while also benefitting employees. Public actors can help companies assess, develop and use their employees' skills. An extensive discussion about the rationale for policy intervention in this area can be found in OECD (2021[7]). To foster in-company provision of career guidance, Germany should consider the following advice:

Target existing programmes for companies to support low-qualified workers: Low-qualified adults are among the groups that are hardest to reach via general career guidance programmes. Existing support programmes for companies should aim to include specific training for and sensitisation of managerial staff on the importance of career guidance for their lower qualified staff. Specific programmes already exist to support companies that lack the capacity to plan training and to provide guidance to their employees. The unternehmensWert: Mensch programme, for example, offers targeted and subsidised consultancy services for SMEs to develop modern, people-centred human resource strategies.

Guidance services for companies should go beyond the initial analysis and recommendations: Enterprises and especially SMEs need support throughout the implementation process. Support with the actual set up of career guidance to employees and later training programmes is crucial to increase take-up.

Strengthen the quality of career guidance services

Career guidance and CET providers have been largely left out of the NWS development process, although their role in the provision of training is crucial. Provider associations should be involved in policy making processes. Working directly with the individuals, it is essential to hear their voice and include their needs in the setup of new programmes. The following steps would be appropriate ways forward to further improve quality:

Implement a nationwide quality standard framework: As described above, this should be an essential component of a common CET guidance brand. Such a framework should cover both the continuous development of a provider's internal processes to further improve the quality of the provision as well as a competency profile for career guidance counsellors, describing the specific expertise that the professionals would ideally have.

Set clear qualification requirements for career guidance counsellors in calls for tender: Currently, many counsellors have no specialised background in career guidance, counselling or adult learning which can undermine the quality of the services they offer. The design of public calls for tenders to choose career guidance providers should include criteria related to the qualifications of career guidance counsellors and their knowledge and expertise in working with (low-qualified) adults, as it is the case e.g. in Berlin's concept paper. This is particularly important when counsellors will be dealing with low-qualified facing multiple barriers. In some countries, it is common for counsellors to be specialised psychologists (see Box 4.4). Besides mandated requirements in calls for tender, better working conditions, notably salaries, can help attract more qualified career counsellors. For example, the latest developments in NRW are a step in the right direction (increasing the hourly allowance, revised quality criteria etc.). Continuity from a user perspective should also be considered when choosing providers, since career guidance for low-qualified adults often depends on long processes of building up trust.

Provide incentives for regular training of career guidance providers: Counsellors working with low-qualified adults are often in a difficult situation aiming to provide career guidance to individuals who are more often than not unaware of guidance and CET options and/ or their benefits, working for employers whose interest in reskilling or upskilling their blue colour workforce is often limited. To be successful, counsellors need to be knowledgeable on all available career guidance and CET programmes and financial incentives as well as on appropriate skills assessments for each individual, but they also to be able to motivate and inspire, clear doubts and open doors. Keeping all these skills up to date requires investment. Some federal states like NRW offer several days of training to new staff, but training should be offered systematically, for example at the co-ordination offices of regional networks or organised by the BA. In the context of the COVID-19 crisis, special focus should be placed on digital skills training. For new hires, the baseline qualification should also be raised and/or specialised on career guidance and working with adults as it is the case in some federal states (Chapters 2 and 3) and other countries (Box 4.4).

Expand the use of AI solutions during the career guidance process: While it is crucial that some components of career guidance are conducted in person by skilled career guidance advisors, others parts of the process could be automated leveraging advances in AI. For instance, initial meetings meant to raise motivation to train are better carried out by a skilled counsellor. Technology can support them when drawing up the user's skills profile while the search of and matching to training and job opportunities could be more easily automated (Verhagen, 2021[8]). As the drop in low-qualified users in Berlin during the COVID-19 crisis confirmed, digital solutions may not always be the best solution for this target group, but e.g. guided use (or co-browsing) can help users become accustomed with the use and strengthen their digital skills.

Box 4.4. Quality standards

BeQu (Beratungsqualität) concept

In Germany the National Guidance Forum of Education and Employment (*Nationales Forum Beratung in Bildung, Beruf und Beschäftigung*, nfb) developed the Guidance Quality Concept. BMBF funded the development of this detailed concept between 2011 and 2014. It includes a quality development framework and a competence profile for career guidance advisors. The concept considers the following dimensions of quality: i) overarching principles, e.g. client orientation, transparency, ethical framework, processes for quality improvement; ii) professionalism and counselling competences; iii) standards relating to the career guidance process; iv) organisational standards; and v) societal objectives and goals. The implementation of a nationwide quality standard framework could be largely based on these standards.

Canada: Competency framework

An example where standards already apply nationwide are the Canadian Standards and Guidelines for Career Development Practitioners (S&G) that outline the competencies needed by the practitioners to provide effective and people-centred guidance across the lifespan. The development of the guidelines was funded by Employment and Social Development Canada (ESDC) along with contributions from career development partners. The objectives in developing these national standards were: to define career development as a legitimate specialisation; to provide a foundation for designing training; to provide quality assurance to the public; to recognise and validate the diverse skill sets of practitioners working in the field; and to create a common voice and vocabulary for career development. The competencies are organised in three areas: core competencies, specialisation competencies and ethical principles.

The concrete implementation can vary by region. To obtain a permit to work as a career counsellor in Quebec (Canada) for example, both a bachelor's and a masters' degree in career counselling must be completed, which include modules on the production and dissemination of labour market information, online sources of labour market information, and how to incorporate labour market information in career counselling.

The Alpha label (*Alphasiegel*)

In Berlin (and Baden-Wuerttemberg) a specific quality label exists for providers who offer their services in an easily accessible way for adults with low literacy. To receive the quality label, at least 20% of the provider's employees need to take part in a half day sensitisation workshop, all communication channels need to be adapted to readers with low literacy (e.g. websites, flyers) and also in the physical spaces of the provider orientation signs need to be accessible to the target group. The development of the label, as well as support for providers during these adaptations are implemented by the Berlin's Senate Department for Education, Youth and Family and the Basic Education Centre (*Grund-Bildungs-Zentrum*) Berlin.

Source: OECD (2021[2]), *Career Guidance for Adults in a Changing World of Work*, https://doi.org/10.1787/9a94bfad-en; OECD (2021[5]), *Continuing Education and Training in Germany*, https://doi.org/10.1787/1f552468-en; Grund-Bildungs-Zentrum Berlin (2021[9]), Bildung für alle. Kompetenz für Berlin., https://grundbildung-berlin.de.

References

BA (2021), *Jugendberufsagenturen: Arbeitsbündnis für bessere Integration Jugendlicher*, http://www.arbeitsagentur.de/institutionen/jugendberufsagenturen. [6]

BVMW (2021), *Bildung in die Mitte der Gesellschaft führen*, http://www.bvmw.de/news/10562/bildung-in-die-mitte-der-gesellschaft-fuehren (accessed on 2021). [1]

CEDEFOP (2021), *How can you integrate LMI in your guidance activities?*, http://www.cedefop.europa.eu/en/tools/resources-guidance/toolkit/how-can-you-integrate-lmi-in-your-guidance-activities. [3]

Centro Qualifica Azambuja (2021), *Centro Qualifica Azambuja*, http://www.facebook.com/centroqualifica.azambuja.3. [4]

Grund-Bildungs-Zentrum Berlin (2021), *Bildung für alle. Kompetenz für Berlin.*, https://grundbildung-berlin.de. [9]

OECD (2021), *Career Guidance for Adults in a Changing World of Work*, Getting Skills Right, OECD Publishing, Paris, https://dx.doi.org/10.1787/9a94bfad-en. [2]

OECD (2021), *Continuing Education and Training in Germany*, Getting Skills Right, OECD Publishing, Paris, https://doi.org/10.1787/1f552468-en. [5]

OECD (2021), *Training in Enterprises: New Evidence from 100 Case Studies*, Getting Skills Right, OECD Publishing, Paris, https://dx.doi.org/10.1787/7d63d210-en. [7]

Verhagen, A. (2021), "Opportunities and drawbacks of using artificial intelligence for training", *OECD Social, Employment and Migration Working Papers*, No. 266, OECD Publishing, Paris, https://dx.doi.org/10.1787/22729bd6-en. [8]

Notes

[1] In Germany, the Employment Agencies (*Agenturen für Arbeit*) provide a wide range of services connected to the labour market and education, such as the payment of compensation benefits, in particular unemployment benefit (*Arbeitslosengeld I, insurance-paid*); placement in jobs and training positions; career counselling, employer counselling; promotion of CET; promotion of the vocational integration of people with disabilities. Besides there are also the job centres, responsible for securing subsistence through unemployment benefit (*Arbeitslosengeld II, tax-paid*), payment of contributions to health and long-term care insurance, accommodation and heating, education and participation benefits, labour market-related integration.

Annex A. Data sources

In Germany there are two institutions collecting data on employment and education: The BA and the statistical offices of the federal states and the federation.

- The **BA** considers employees only, excluding self-employed and civil servants. The employment statistics of the BA record the employment relationships based on the employers' social insurance reports for individuals aged 15-64. Information on vocational qualifications is only available for around 89% of employees subject to social insurance contributions in Germany. The resulting uncertainty must be taken into account when considering the extent and distribution of different educational backgrounds. The group of low-qualified persons are to be understood as those employees who: (i) do not have a vocational qualification for which a training period of at least two years is stipulated under federal or federal state law, or (ii) have a vocational qualification but have worked in a semi-skilled or unskilled job for more than four years, which makes them be considered to no longer be likely to be able to work in their profession (occupationally alienated).

- The **statistical offices of the federal states and the federation** conduct the annual micro census, following the labour force concept of the ILO: All persons aged 15 years or older who are employed as employees (blue-collar and white-collar workers subject to compulsory social insurance employees incl. trainees, civil servants, marginally employed persons, soldiers and those doing those doing community service) or as self-employed persons and family members helping out are engaged in an activity aimed at economic gain, irrespective of the extent of this activity. Following the ILO concept, an unemployed person is any person aged 15 to 74 who was not in employment during the reference week, but who had been actively seeking employment during the four weeks preceding the interview. The micro census uses international standards to define low-qualified adults: The definition includes all adults who have less than primary, primary and lower secondary education, ISCED levels 0-2. As opposed to the BA's definition, these adults do not have a higher education entrance qualification (*Hochschulreife*).

The report also draws from **qualitative interviews on career guidance (QIG)** commissioned specifically for this study. The German Institute for Adult Education (DIE) conducted these interviews with 50 low-qualified employees with the objective to learn directly from them about their experiences with and their barriers towards the use of career guidance. Half of the interviewees are female, they are between 18 and 59 years old, 40% had a migration background and 40% lived in a rural area. Sixty percent of them have used career guidance services and reported their experiences, while the other 40% reported on their barriers towards using training (see Annex B).

Annex B. Methodology note on the qualitative interviews with low-qualified employees

This report uses data collected in the 2021 qualitative interviews on career guidance with low-qualified employees (QIG). The QIG was conducted to better understand the experience of low-qualified employees with career guidance services, as well as the barriers they face towards using them and to shed light on underlying explanations of available quantitative data.

Fieldwork was conducted by the German Institute for Adult Education (*Deutsches Institut für Erwachsenenbildung,* DIE) using a questionnaire developed by the OECD. It took place from mid-September to November 2021 in Germany. The interviews were conducted face-to-face wherever possible and otherwise via videoconference tools or phone.

The questionnaire covered the following topics: i) information on the interviewee, such as the quotas described above, the employment situation and aspirations, ii) initiation of the guidance and barriers, iii) time, place and provider, iv) details on the received service, v) satisfaction with the received service.

The sample was restricted to adults aged 18-64, in order to target those who had left initial education while looking at a broad range of information on younger, middle-aged and older employees. The DIE conducted the interviews with 50 adults using a stratified sample methodology, which imposed quotas on:

- **Qualification**: Adults whose highest educational attainment level is at most lower secondary education (ISCED 0-2) (*Geringqualifizierte*). In the German context, these adults have left education after compulsory comprehensive school or earlier (*Primär- und Sekundarbereich I*) and at most hold a secondary school certificate (*Realschulabschluss/ Mittlere Reife*). They have not completed a full vocational qualification.
- **Employment status**: All adults are in employment.
- **Age**: All adults are between 18-64 years old
- **Gender**: Half of the adults are female and half are male
- **Migration background**: Ca. 15 adults have a migration background.
- **Whether the adult has used career guidance**: Ca. half of the adults have used career guidance.
- **Occupations**: All adults are employed in one of the following occupations. These are the occupations (ISCO 08 – 2 digits) that are most threatened by automation in Germany, according to PIAAC.

IC technicians	Food preparation assistants
Market-oriented skilled agricultural workers	Sales workers
Metal, machinery & related trades workers	Legal, social, cultural & related associate prof.
Electrical & electronic trades workers	Refuse workers & other elementary workers
Handicraft & printing workers	Agricultural, forestry & fishery labourers
Building & related trades workers, excl. electricians	Cleaners & helpers
Food processing, wood working, other craft & trades workers	Drivers and mobile plant operators
Assemblers	Labourers in mining, construction, manufacturing & transport

Glossary

Continuing education and training (CET) is learning undertaken by adults who have already completed their initial education and training and entered working life. **Job-related CET** helps adults to acquire new skills, in order to retrain, change career, increase their employability and for their professional development. CET can also be non-job related, i.e. for personal development, but this is not the focus of this report.

CET includes formal and non-formal education and training, as well as informal learning:

- **Formal education and training** opportunities are intentional, institutionalised learning activities, which are recognised by relevant authorities and have a minimum duration of one semester. Examples include upper secondary qualifications or Bachelor degree studies.
- **Non-formal education and training** includes intentional, institutionalised learning activities (e.g. short courses, workshops and seminars) which are either of short duration (less than one semester) or not recognised by the relevant authorities.
- **Informal learning** is intentional learning, which is non-institutionalised, less structured than formal and non-formal learning and can take place anywhere. Examples of informal learning include learning from colleagues, friends or learning by doing.

Guidance services for continuing education and training help individuals to make educational, training and occupational choices. As well as providing information, they typically offer counselling, mentoring and/or skills assessment.

Low-qualified adults can be defined either as individuals aged 25-64 whose highest educational attainment level is at most lower secondary education (ISCED 0-2), or, as often done in the German context, as individuals not having completed a formal vocational training (see also Annex A). For information on low-skilled adults in Germany (according to PIAAC and the LEO study) see OECD (2021[1]).

Partial qualifications are building blocks of full qualifications. They can be acquired either to build a full qualification over time, or specialisation or skills updating. Partial qualifications require assessment and validation to certify the learning outcomes an individual has achieved, and usually include a form of official recognition.

Qualifications are the formal outcome of an assessment and validation process, obtained when a competent authority or body determines that an individual has achieved learning outcomes according to given standards. The outcome can be a degree, diploma or other certificate. A qualification can also be a legal entitlement to practice a trade.

Validation is a process of confirming that an individual has acquired skills measured against a relevant standard. This process is conducted by an authorised body.

References

OECD (2021), *Continuing Education and Training in Germany*, Getting Skills Right, OECD Publishing, Paris, https://doi.org/10.1787/1f552468-en.   [1]